After gaining independence from Spain in the 1820s, Guatemala had a long history of government by authoritarian rule and military regimes until it came under democratic rule in 1985. Starting in 1954, Guatemala's governments faced formidable guerrilla opposition that sparked civil war that lasted for 36 years until peace accords were signed in 1996.

A slow political and economic recovery continued into the early 21st century. Elections have been held regularly since 1996, but, because there are many political parties, which tend to be small and short-lived, convergence on political solutions has been rare.

Although it is difficult for some to accept, Guatemala is the main economic power in Central America, but despite its high production and its many exports, the wealth is owned by a small group, politicians and businessmen who finance their campaigns. Poverty, strict religion and little access to education delay cultural, scientific and social progress.

The birth of the State of Guatemala derives from the interests of the dominant groups to promote the emancipation of the Spanish Crown and, thus, maintain the status quo. This was consolidated in the 19th century with the formation of a liberal State, which created a patrimonial model, destined to protect the privileges of the elite, already in contemporary times and after the peace accords that in 1996 put an end to a war of 40-year-old guerrillas, a weakened State allowed the emergence of a new class whose aim is the plunder of the State through harmful businesses, with drug trafficking as a common denominator.

Ejecting these groups from power will not be an easy task, but now there is a social awareness that can mark the beginning of change. Citizen exercise becomes an uphill battle when

democracy is hijacked, with billions of dollars circulating each campaign. However, the fed-up citizen managed to oust the Government of General Otto Pérez in September 2015, the same spirit that they have maintained in every demonstration since that date.

But is a demonstration enough to end corruption?

Corruption does not only affect the economy of the poorest families, but the integral development of the country, and that is more necessary for the development of a country but a good maintenance and use of natural resources and the environment. So the question arises, why is Guatemala such a dirty country with such great natural wealth? Is it just the responsibility of political mismanagement? Is it just the result of corruption? Or is it the reflection of a decadent society?

Guatemala has one of the largest and most impressive fauna of the American continent, it is one of the countries that, together with Mexico, exports tons of products to the countries of North America, Asia and Europe. However, there is not in that country, a single river, beach, or lake, clean, in addition to the solid waste that people discharge in the streets, industrial waste, the common factor in water bodies is the discharge of fecal waste. raw. Both urban areas, larger cities, rural areas and people who live on the banks of rivers, seas or lakes, discharge the contents of the toilet directly into the water, without any type of previous treatment and without any shame.

One of the largest lakes in Guatemala, and in Central America, is Lake Amatitlan, surrounded by mountains, it crosses 14 municipalities, is only 20 minutes from the capital and is completely abandoned. According to the National Aeronautics and

Space Administration (NASA), the pollution of the lakes of Guatemala is visible from space.

Amatitlan is the lake of eternal discord, a resource that seems to have more value if it remains contaminated. Every year the administration acquires millionaire contracts for the supposed cleaning of the lake, from aeration and magic water to eliminate the contamination, to fountains with colored lights that do not alleviate the agony of the wounded lake at all.

Source: Prensa Libre (2000)

Source: Prensa Libre (2015)

Lake Amatitlán is doomed to die. For more than twenty years it has faced three phenomena that could dry it up and cause its disappearance in the not too distant future, a catastrophe that will have a strong ecological and social impact. The entry of water pollution from drains (or wastewater) of fourteen municipalities that make up the basin; the entry of sediments such as sand, earth and others; and finally the entry of solid waste, they are killing one of the largest lakes with a little exploited tourist attraction in Guatemala. The people who live around the lake and who are engaged in fishing or tourism, have suffered a severe blow to their economy, since pollution has caused a reduction in the population of fish, and in the flow of visitors.

César Castañeda Salguero, researcher at the Institute of Natural Resources and Agriculture (IARNA) of the Rafael Landívar University (URL), made an analysis of the relationship between society and the environment, and how one transforms the other.

"To exert changes in the environment, say decontamination of lakes, rivers, among others, a change is necessary in the national policy that allows the development of the Guatemalan; that guarantees access to health, education, employment, land, among other basic needs. What is called integral development ", *highlighted.*

The Lake Amatitlán Authority, AMSA, was created in September 1996, and according to the media and published reports, from 1998 to 2017 AMSA has received close to Q500 million in operating budget and loans with the Inter-American Development Bank (IDB) between 2008 to 2015; however, its progress has been nil. The lamentable state of Lake Amatitlán is a consequence of the lack of laws that require the proper use of water, the elimination of municipal landfills, the implementation of water recharges in urban areas and the corruption in which said institution has been involved.

But not only does it economically affect fishermen and vendors in the area, pollution also has an impact on people's physical and mental health, and this alters the social conditions of the entire country. Poor environmental conditions cause a negative impact on the individuals that make up the social group, they are involved in a vicious circle in which, seeing the little interest and the use of political actors, collective psychology turns into frustration that It results in a lack of interest and involvement in environmental issues. The environment and its problematic manifestations constitute, according to the qualifier of the French psychology professor Michel-Louis Rouquette, "a major object of social psychology." Generally approached as an object of social representations, the environment constitutes the ideological framework of a group of sub-objects (environmental quality, environmental risks, ecological behaviors).

According to the World Health Organization (WHO), health is "the state of complete physical, mental and social well-being and not just the mere absence of disease", which is directly affected and influenced by the environment and the environment in which we live. Therefore, environmental pollution can be defined as any undesirable modification of the environment, caused by the introduction of physical, chemical or biological agents (pollutants) in quantities greater than those found in the natural state, causing damage to natural resources and altering the balance. ecological, deriving all this in harmful results for human health.

Two experts from the Institute of Psychiatry at King's College London, identified the potential risks of climate change that would affect mental health:

-Natural disasters (floods, droughts, cyclones) are increasing as a result of climate change, causing adverse psychiatric disorders in people. Among them are post-traumatic stress, severe depression or somatoform disorders.

-Temperatures are getting higher and higher due to air pollution, being people with mental illnesses especially vulnerable to the danger of death related to heat. Suicides could also increase from a temperature threshold.

-The needs of people with chronic mental illness are often overlooked when major events occur, as psychological interventions are intended for individuals who have just suffered trauma; increasing the risk of mortality or deterioration of the mentally ill.

-The changes of residence is another aspect of climate change that affects the mental health of the population derived from coastal changes and the increase in floods, which give rise to mass migration and displacement. Although urbanization could be beneficial on the one hand (it increases the possibilities of work and access to health services), it is being associated with an increase in the incidence of schizophrenia in developed countries.

Stress is a response of living beings to adapt to the changing conditions of the environment and makes us alert when we perceive a danger, or it adapts us to carry out a certain activity. When the response capacity or resistance to stress is exceeded by the intensity or duration of the aggression, a chronic state of neuroendocrinological defense occurs and a subsequent exhaustion by not being able to withstand that intensity of reaction for so long, giving rise to mental illnesses. Environmental pollution as a form of stressful situation causes decreased concentration, increases anxiety and depression, and sleep disorders. People become more irritable or aggressive.

Some recent research has shown that long-term exposure to polluted air causes an acceleration in cognitive deterioration, finding that women who in areas with poorer air quality obtained lower results in memory and reasoning tests; Because such exposure contributes to a two-year decline in normal brain function, which could lead to an early onset of Alzheimer's-type mental illnesses. Another study in Germany found that people who lived near busy roads performed worse on tests of memory and reasoning than people in rural areas. It is true that it is difficult to establish a direct relationship between environmental toxins and Alzheimer's dementias, since there are many factors involved. But other studies like the ones above have linked air pollution to an increased risk of stroke and cardiovascular disease. Likewise, circulatory and vascular problems have also been linked to dementia.

The San Francisco de Asís Hospital in Spain published a study on the relationship between contamination and the risk of mental pathologies in which it explained that contamination increased the risk of neurological pathologies, anxiety and depression; and that a good part of health depended on a strong immune system, which is the one that has the capacity to protect the body against diseases. Impairment of the immune system as a result of sustained exposure to a polluted environment causes the alteration of the body's cellular and humoral reactive capacity, resulting in an alteration of the immune defenses and therefore increasing the possibilities of mental illnesses.

The IV International Virtual Congress of Mental Health Nursing, in 2018, concluded that; Although it is true that the development of mental illnesses can probably have a genetic predisposition, but for such affectation to occur, the intervention of causal or triggering factors of the disease is necessary. Dumping large amounts of harmful elements into the environment produces

serious balance problems in natural systems. The current
increase in mental illness seems to be a response of the body to
the negative influence of these pollutants in the air, especially
over long periods. These data show that environmental pollution
plays a much more important role than we thought in the
production or aggravation of diseases.
Scientists warn of the need to carry out more and better research
on the mechanisms by which climate change causes the
appearance of mental illnesses, and thus be able to face
problems from this perspective. If we all collaborate in reducing
pollution, we would improve the quality of life and the
conservation of our planet.

When the Lake Amatitlán basin takes its rightful place as one of
the most important places in Central America, we will see far-
reaching effects and wonder why it took so long?

To work on the recovery of the Lake and avoid the increase in the
effects that have caused the worst human error, the Guatemalan
Congress must deactivate AMSA, it must convert all tenants along
the lake into land ownership with clear titles , including full rights
therein and must declare the land on the lake as a special
economic zone in which citizens in the lake can choose to tax
their real estate capital gains. Once these three changes have
been implemented, the technical response to clean up Lake
Amatitlán should be to treat the flow of the Villalobos River.

REVIVE AMATITLAN: THE COMPARATIVE PILOT THAT AMSA EVOID

"FORMER AMSA ADMINISTRATIONS HAVE PREFERRED TO IMPROVISE PROJECTS RATHER THAN CARRYING OUT A SCIENTIFIC STUDY TO DETERMINE WHICH IS THE MOST COST-EFFICIENT TECHNOLOGY TO REDUCE LAKE POLLUTION. THE REASON? THE PROBLEM IS GOING AND SO IS THE CORRUPTION ..."
-May 30, 2019 PERRO BRAVO MAGAZINE -

In 2019, I published a video that has generated thousands of reactions and comments on social networks, which describes how I and a group of foreign citizens who were trying to carry out a pilot to apply a technology of American origin in Lake Amatitlán, we were intimidated by armed guards who worked for the Authority for the Sustainable Management of the Lake Amatitlan Basin (AMSA), when we tried to remove our equipment after seeing the pilot blocked that could have offered a point of scientific comparison with other available technologies to clean the water.

The answer that has circulated in networks by Amed Juárez Sosa, the then director of AMSA, removed a few months ago from his position, is that the statement is "completely false", that the equipment offered was based on a cavitation process and that the «Investigations by biologists with experience of the institution determined that there was no such cavitation process, verifying that the devices called by them cavitators were simple« aerators ». Juárez adds that "an institutional technical report was generated by Biologist Manuel Cano, in charge of the AMSA laboratory, where such an extreme was demonstrated."
What Juárez Sosa forgets to mention is the onerous new plan to save the lake that he authorized in collusion with Vice President

Jafeth Cabrera, without having any point of comparison with other projects and technologies, in terms of cost and efficiency and, more importantly, , that he
«These are times of electoral politics and many want to hold on anything. If they have evidence of what they accuse me of reportin me to the Public Ministry, I only know that I did the right thing. "

The biologist he refers to as the head of the laboratory, Manuel Cano, was working in that same institution when the implementation of the popularly known "magic water" was authorized with which Roxana Baldetti and her associates sought to obtain illicitly several million from AMSA's budget, deceiving shamelessly to the population. Where was the professional rigor of Cano and the AMSA laboratory back then?

The new business starts with the land
With the same fury with which Baldetti defended the hiring of the "magic" formula, the current Vice President, Jafeth Cabrera, promotes the new plan to clean up Lake Amatitlán. "A large project is planned, the highest cost is the purchase of the land, with a number of hectares that allows diverting all the rivers that arrive contaminated ... It is estimated that 150 million quetzals could be spent to buy that land, there it is it would build a treatment plant, which is an obligation of mayors but has never been done... "Cabrera explained to the national. According to AMSA authorities, the plan called "Construction of the Lagoon System and Artificial Wetland for Tertiary Treatment", which would be built at the mouth of the Villalobos River,

Without any scientific support or evidence to prove its effectiveness, since if they exist they have not been publicly shared as endorsement of the project, citizens have to settle for a promotional video that presents fictitious images of what the project would look like.

It would include: a conduction channel for the capture of the Villalobos river towards the lagoon, a solid waste capture grid, a sand trap, covered anaerobic lagoons to capture methane gas (biogas), energy generators with biogas, facultative lagoons, pipes for water venting, oxidation ponds, aerators for water oxygenation, artificial wetland for phyto-purification, a bamboo plantation, an iguanarium, sludge drying yard, greenhouses, forest nurseries, solid waste recycling area, a heliport, area of trainings and extensive parking.

Of course, everything described above cannot be executed in the current administration, so the negotiation of the land is the main objective of AMSA's current management.

Some sources close to AMSA and Lake Amatitlan, reported that since September 2018, representatives of the Office for the Control of Territorial Reserve Areas of the State (OCRET), have been pressuring those who own the right titles of various lands around the lake, so that negotiate them with "interested third parties". Likewise, sources close to the Vice Presidency confirm that Cabrera has held meetings with the director of OCRET in relation to the AMSA project. It should be remembered that the director of OCRET is Juan Carlos Ovalle, son of one of the founders of FCN-Nación, a deputy and currently a fugitive from justice for the Creompaz case, Edgar Ovalle.

AMSA, without presenting any comparative table to the public, assures that "the lagoon system is the cheapest in the market", and that "this ensures that it works by gravity without the need for electricity or fuel to pump the water." The institution affirms that

around "120 blocks will be necessary for the construction ", which will be carried out in phases and" we could start in 2019 ".
In September 2018, Amed Juárez, director of AMSA, presented the final draft of the new plan to clean up the lake to the Vice Presidency. The content of the file has not been made public to date.

Bet on a new project without credibility.
In response to the announcement of the new plan and its promotional video, social networks have shown rejection and skepticism, making a comparison with the fraud perpetrated by Roxana Baldetti and the AMSA authorities at the time.

The user Victoria Bárbara thinks that "years later, it turns out that the work was overrated and also left unfinished, the contractors by pure chance turned out to be relatives of the politician who authorized it, and years later they are imprisoned. Not without first going through a lengthy trial, in the end the money was stolen and it is almost impossible to get it back ... Anyway, the same old story. "

Citizen Kevin Luna also commented on the video: "It seems that this will be the case of Agua Mágica # 2, it is well known that corruption in Guatemala continues and it seems to me that even Baldetti contributed so that this administration can once again steal on a large scale. I hope that those who see this video are not fooled... ".

One of the reasons why the public's rejection of the project is manifested is that, once again, the authorities intend to justify a multimillion-dollar investment, without first demonstrating reliably, through a pilot, that the proposed measures work, that the evidence Scientists establish that these are the options with the best results and the highest cost efficiency. The participation of any university in the planning of the project.

For the American who proposed the preflight model, it is clear that AMSA managers preferred to campaign, rather than favor science in decision-making. "We proposed to them the cultivation of bamboo and the capture of methane to generate energy. They still do not understand, it will not work as they are presenting it. The degree of contamination in the flow of the rivers is insufficient to produce abundant methane, the highest concentration is found in the decades of accumulated sludge at the bottom of the lake, but they cannot or do not want to understand it ", says Douglas Lewis.

Before continuing to invest millions, it is the duty of the Guatemalan authorities to scientifically demonstrate the technology that can eliminate each kilo of contamination.
At the end of the AMSA spot presenting the new project, it shows an area view highlighting that its design is in the shape of a mojarra, a symbolism that reminds us of the Baldetti hoax.

More information was sought with Erick Barcárcel, AMSA spokesperson, but did not communicate back, and no further details of the project, much less the baseline studies, are published on the official AMSA website.

"After hundreds of millions invested in the rescue of the lake through AMSA, without yielding positive results in its 22 years of existence, the rulers continue with the folly of presenting projects, without first showing the population that this is the right investment at a lower cost. " Douglas Lewis, American businessman
Politicians are not interested in solving the problem, because the source of income is ending. It is better for them to perpetuate the disease than to allow science to heal it. They fail to understand

the message of 2015, which was precisely Baldetti's blatant ruse to defend the corrupt business on the lake that ignited the outrage of citizens.

After this investigation was made public and my video received so much attention, the deputies of the UNE bench invited me to a speech with the AMSA employees and the promoters of the last opaque and evidence-free project that they intended to carry out. The result of this intervention was the indefinite interruption of this project.

But the fight between the environment and corruption is not limited to Lake Amatitlan, parallel to my publications on Lake Amatitlan and AMSA. I also investigated the anomalous "investment", meaningless and without any technical or scientific support from the Development Fund -FODES-, a doubtful investment of Q107 million, destined to purchase 300 prefabricated water treatment plants, but without specifying in which areas of the country will be installed.
According to a source within the FODES, there are precepts of senior managers of that institution to make purchases that do not meet the specifications between the contract and the bidding rules.

This purchase became effective in July 2019 and the company "Mercadeo del Agua SA" -MERCAGUA- received more than US $13 million for 138 prefabricated wastewater treatment plants, supposedly for six regions of the country. According to the bidding board, MERCAGUA exactly met the qualification criteria; "price, experience, delivery time and guarantee", for which it obtained 94.9 points. It is unknown if the plants have been installed or if they really work.

MERCAGUA, is represented by Juan Carlos Paiz Gomez and Oscar Gilberto Paiz Ramirez, according to the Guatemalan Government's electronic purchasing portal -GUATECOMPRAS-, where it also appears that since 2004, MERCAGUA has been awarded 133 contracts for more than US $ 35 million.

Paiz Gomez, coincidentally, is a known name in the Prosecutor's Office Against Corruption of the Public Ministry, he has an international arrest warrant since 2016 for his alleged participation in a corruption case. According to the prosecution, the authorizations of the Development Unit for Popular Housing -UDEVIPO- authorized a project in Chinautla that was not carried out.

The Paiz Gomez also have a link with the VAMOS party, yes, the one with which the current president Alejandro Giammattei won the elections. Although Victor Hugo Paiz Gomez is a minority financier of the political organization, he topped the list of congressmen for the Zacapa district. he, too, was mayor of Teculutan, in the same district, for two terms, the first with the UNE-GANA alliance and the last in 2012 with the civic committee "El Zapato".

Camilo Dedet, secretary of the VAMOS party, confirmed the participation of Victor Hugo within the group, as coordinator of the Zacapa district.

The Paiz Gomez brothers have participated in politics for several periods. Cesar Augusto, was a congressman in Zacapa for two persuasions and was a member of various political organizations such as the MLN and PAN, he closed his term as governor between 2004 and 2008.

The family denied knowing Juan Carlos, one of the MERCAGUA representatives. According to Victor Hugo, they are "the only Paiz Gomez in Zacapa" and they don't know "any Juan Carlos."
This completely anomalous investment was carried out without anyone noticing, no other authority above FODES, no prosecutor, not the congress, nor the population said anything. More than US $ 13 million was spent without any explanation, money that is not going to come back.

If we look again at Lake Amatitlan

Since the Authority for the Sustainable Management of the Lake Amatitlán Basin -AMSA- was assigned a budget for its operation, the institution has invested Q1 thousand 877 million in projects for the sanitation of Lake Amatitlán. However, environmentalists question the success of the actions stating that the real causes of the contamination of the basin are not attacked.

According to the Expense Management and Execution Reports transferred by AMSA corresponding to the period 2004-2014, the total amount of investment in programs and technical policies to reduce pollutants that affect Lake Amatitlán, its tributary basins and the water table, amounts to Q1.87 billion.

According to the entity, the various disbursements in 10 years respond to projects of environmental education, urban planning and land use, operation and maintenance, as well as control, quality and management of water resources in the place; although the total expenditures were not broken down with precision.
The same source announced that the population that lives in the 14 municipalities that make up the Lake Amatitlán basin is 2 million 623 thousand 389 people for 2014, but it is estimated that around 15 thousand people live on the shores of this system water.

AMSA also pointed out that the municipalities that dump the most waste into the Lake are Villa Nueva, Villa Canales, Mixco, San Miguel Petapa, Santa Catarina Pinula, as well as the southern part of Guatemala City and the settlements located on the banks. Finally, the government institution reported that in the basin there are some 900 industries in different areas such as textile, metallurgical, food, chemical, plastic, rubber and rubber, wood, plaster and ceramics, but only 32% of the companies carry out a treatment of its waters, generating 1,500 tons of sediment per day in the lake body, 60,300 cubic meters a day of sewage, and the extraction of 618,000 square meters of garbage annually.

In December 2009, during the government of President Álvaro Colom, AMSA installed 40 oxygenators in the depth of Lake Amatitlán to reduce the amount of sedimentation and planted a million trees in the surroundings in an attempt to recover the basin. Q66 million were invested in the project, according to official sources, although currently only eight oxygenators work. The controversy persists over the purchase of a "magic formula" that AMSA awarded, through two contracts for Q137.8 million and that they assure will clean Lake Amatitlán in less than 10 months.

The payment without support of Q11 million 361 thousand 305 for the rental of machinery is added to the indications of irregular businesses in the Authority for the Sustainable Management of the Lake Amatitlán Basin (Amsa), after the "magic formula" to decontaminate the Lago, which keeps about 15 people in prison.

The new signal is for the rental of machinery without the option to purchase for work on the sanitary landfill located at kilometer 22 of Bárcenas, Villa Nueva. According to the audit report of the Comptroller General of Accounts (CGC), director Edvin Francisco Ramos Soberanis - in prison for fraud and breach of duties - would have signed the contract for night work in the landfill.

The agreement was from February 11 to August 26, 2015. Although the contracted amount was Q11.9 million, it was rescinded and Amsa paid only Q11 million 361 thousand 305 to the company Maquinaria y Constructora Palacios, Sociedad Anónima.

On October 27, the authorities rented trucks for 947 trips within the landfill for Q89,965, with the company Consultora y Constructora del Sur, owned by Maynor Arturo Palacios Muñoz, who was a representative of the first company mentioned. The CGC report revealed that Amsa did not publish any bidding process prior to awarding the contract in February, but until August 26, and did so as a lease by exception. "It reflects a lack of transparency, inconsistencies and deficiencies," indicates the CGC.

No evidence

The supervision reports for the payment to the company were signed by former technical deputy director Juan Díaz Sandoval. The documents state that it was night work to receive trucks with material from a private company with which Amsa signed a contract indicated not to meet requirements, according to CGC. The record of entry of trucks and machinery work does not exist at night. The auditors requested reports and the authorities indicated that they found no documents.

Since 2015, the Villa Nueva Criminal First Instance judge tied 15 people to the trial, including former Vice President Roxana Baldetti and her brother Mario Baldetti, linked to a structure that sought to obtain the project concession in an irregular manner. Sanitation of Lake Amatitlán.

The cleaning project, according to investigations by the Public Ministry, was valued at Q137.8 million, of which Q22.8 million was advanced to the Israeli company M. Tarcic Engineering LTD, by a formula that after different laboratory tests turned out to be water with salt.

That the garbage extraction service is charged directly in the single property tax (IUSI) or in the electric power bill is a proposal of the Authority for the Sustainable Management of the Amatitlán Basin and Lake (Amsa), for the municipalities with influence in that lake body.

To determine the viability of the initiative, Amsa sent a request for consultation to the Constitutional Court
(CC), through the General Secretariat of the Presidency, which received it last Friday and must give it the corresponding process. Óscar Amed Juárez, former executive director of Amsa, stated that if they get a positive response from the CC, they should start looking for a way to integrate the Q25 or Q30 rate for the extraction service into one of the two mandatory fees paid by residents of those municipalities.

In this way they pretend that the payment is unavoidable, in order to avoid clandestine landfills or that the waste is thrown into the rivers that flow into the lake.
Amsa filed 18 complaints with the Public Ministry. Three were against textile companies, two against poultry industries and two for food products, in addition to a shopping center, and 10 against individuals.

The actions were taken because these businesses do not have sanitation processes, despite the fact that there is a law that requires their incorporation.

With the Amsa authorities, some 50 companies have come to present curative and non-preventive solutions for Lake Amatitlán, mainly for residual problems and the sanitary landfill. Offerings include bacteria, oxygen and waste treatment; however, the offers amount to up to US $ 400 million.

In Lake Atitlan:

Authorities have begun actions in the lake to avoid further contamination by sewage.

In 2009, the first cyanobacterial outbreak was detected, which is estimated to be reversible until 2019.

The current big problems are the entry of sewage, nutrients, sediments and chemicals, solid waste and leachate.

There are 14 water treatment plants around the lake. But none is on.

They have identified 264 clandestine garbage dumps.

About one hundred thousand people consume the lake's water.

The authorities implement awareness workshops.

In Lake Amatitlan:

Authorities have also begun actions in Lake Atitlán to prevent further contamination by wastewater.

It is the most polluted lake. There are already criminal actions against companies for dumping waste without controls.

Diagnostics have described the quality of the water as bad, close to becoming appalling.

The lake is polluted by between 1,600 and 2,000 liters of water every second, which arrive with toxic waste and garbage.

There are nine treatment plants. But none is on.

18 complaints have been filed against companies and a shopping center, for not treating the water that discard from their collectors.

The current big problems are the entry of sewage, nutrients, sediments and chemicals, solid waste and leachate.

What is Revive Amatitlan and why was it blocked?

Revive Amatitlán is an environmental project that was born out of the need for transparency in the cleaning and investment of Lake Amatitlán and Guatemala's natural resources, which proposes a comparative pilot project that facilitates cleanup work and determines the real cost of its recovery; with the aim of recovering the beauty of Lake Amatitlán and making the management of municipal resources in the basin sustainable. In this short chronological story, we narrate the way in which the local authorities blocked Revive Amatitlán. It is not a 100 percent scientific report.

The Lake Amatitlán It has a history as beautiful as it is sad, it is a crater lake located in Guatemala, its formation is due to the tecto-volcanic movements that occurred in the area and caused by the volcanoes of Pacaya, Agua, Fuego and Acatenango.

The meaning of the word Amat it lán, Der iva etymologically from the Nahuatl language is an agglutinated place name that is structured in the following way:
• Amatl = "Amate "or" Amatle "(Ficus Glabrata).
• Titlan = "between "or" surrounded "

Administratively the lake is located within the Guatemala Department, However, inside the lake is the administrative division of the municipalities Villa Nueva, Villa Canales, San Miguel Petapa and Amatitlán, Therefore, each of these municipalities have part of the lake within their jurisdiction, in addition the lake basin is made up of 14 municipalities, 7 of them directly influence the lake due to the degradation of natural resources, these being: Villa Nueva City, Villa Canales, Santa Catarina Pinula, San Miguel Petapa, Mixco City, Amatitlán, and zones 11, 12 and 21 of Guatemala City.

The population of the basin is more than 2 million inhabitants; Villa Nueva being the most populated municipality. With an altitude of 1,188 meters above sea level, it is 12 km long, 3 km wide, and a surface area of 15.2 km2, and it is the fourth largest body of water in the Central American country. Its maximum depth was 33 meters, but currently its average depth is 14 meters with a reduction trend of 1 meter per year. The volume of the body of water is approximately 0.286 km3.

The Villalobos River, which feeds the lake, is one of the main sewage drains for domestic, industrial and agro-industrial waters of the metropolitan area of Guatemala City. Every year a significant volume of sewage and 500,000 cubic meters of sedimententer the lake. This situation has resulted in high levels of contamination and accelerated eutrophication and sedimentation, affecting the lake's functions as a source of drinking water, for fishing and irrigation, and has reduced its recreational functions.

AMSA with the purpose of protecting and recovering the Lake of Ama titlán, mediate decontamination and the rational use of renewable and non-renewable resources in aquifer recharge zones and forested areas. AMSA is made up of an executive and administrative division, a solid waste management division, a liquid waste management division and a forestry division.

Although the creation of AMSA was a laudable initiative, in 24 years of existence, it has not achieved any improvement in the management of natural resources, or in reducing pollution.
The American scientist and businessman Douglas Lewis, owner of the company Wastewater Alchemy Inc., settled years ago in Guatemala to study the problem of water pollution, drawing his interest in the serious situation of Lake Amatitlán. In 2015, I met the initiative, and I joined it.

After the change of government, after the citizen demonstrations of 2015, hoping that corruption would recede, Lewis decides to approach the new administration of AMSA, to present an innovative technology that, by creating an ecosystem that favors the growth of an organism called archaea, allows to eliminate contamination in the water and sludge at the bottom of the lake. The plan proposed by Lewis suggested using a system of natural lagoons that are connected, just where the Villalobos river flows, one of the main polluting factors of the lake, which allowed to dispense with the construction of huge treatment plants, which have proven over the years that their results are insufficient to solve the problem and generate high operating costs.

However, Lewis's approach, with the support of the "Ciudadanos por el Agua" collective, was not hiring the Wastewater Alchemy Inc. teams, but rather conducting scientific tests that would allow for comparison between this and other technologies. in order to establish the relationship between efficiency and costs.

"The most practical way to compare the efficiency of the available technologies is to measure the reduction of the Chemical Oxygen Demand (COD), which is the necessary amount of oxygen that is required to oxidize the organic and oxidizable matter present in water. residual ", Lewis explains," that is why we proposed that, before investing any amount of public money, it be demonstrated through a pilot plan, what is the best solution to clean Lake Amatitlán ".

Eng. Amed Juárez, at the moment executive director of AMSA, and Douglas Lewis, signed an agreement of understanding for the realization of free tests with this modern technology, for the reduction of contamination, algae and sludge, as well as to make the monitoring of the results transparent, so that an objective comparison could be made between the yields of the different treatments offered to clean the lake's waters.

In November 2016, without using public money, Douglas Lewis along with a group of volunteers, installed two cavitation machines to start the pilot in the waters of the lake, in the area known as Playa Oro, a few meters from where the sewage enters. from the Villalobos river.

Perro Bravo Magazine was invited to document the pilot test, so 1 week after the equipment began to function, this medium carried out the management for Laboratorios Labind, a private initiative, to carry out a sampling and subsequent analysis, with the purpose of independently obtaining data on Chemical Oxygen Demand (COD), as well as BOD5 analysis, microbiology and Dissolved Oxygen, in the area under study.

As recorded in AMSA's history, the lowest COD record in the same area, at that time, had been 20.5 mg / L, and the highest was 73 mg / L. The results of the first laboratory tests were overwhelming: COD levels dropped to 4.5 mg / L, just one week after the machines were running.

Despite the fact that in the agreement signed between the institution and Lewis, it is established that "AMSA agrees to take COD samples three to four times a week, and to map the depth of the mud and estimate the density of the mud at least Once a week ", and that" AMSA accepts that the results of these analyzes and measurements will be made public in their entirety and at the time the results are available "; in practice, AMSA did its best to evade that commitment.

Only before the is tence of the North American business, and before the request of the data by this medium, AMSA carried out the first analyzes unilaterally and without public support. The weekly COD analyzes were not carried out, nor was the constant mapping of sludge carried out by the institution.

On the contrary, the relationship between Douglas Lewis and the AMSA authorities deteriorated. The electrical current that fed the equipment began to be cut repeatedly, preventing a full week from running uninterruptedly for the respective sampling by third parties, such as universities or independent laboratories. When reporting the situation, as well as acts of vandalism against the equipment, the AMSA authorities limited themselves to attributing them to problems with the electric power service and security, beyond their reach.

Another important aspect to evaluate was the energy consumption represented by this technology, for which reason a clause was also included in the agreement that established that "on a constant basis, AMSA agrees to measure, record and make public the Kwh consumed for each kilogram of COD reduced and per Kg. Of sludge removed, and make decisions about potential future acquisitions, based on these two metrics ", which was also not met by the institution's authorities, evidencing their unwillingness to make scientific comparisons to support any plan.

CAVITATION: A possible solution?

Cavitation is a phenomenon that appears in liquids when the pressure drops below the liquid vapor pressure at the existing temperature. As a consequence of cavitation, vaporization nuclei appear that can appear in the form of bubbles, pockets, or both. Revive Amatitlán's proposal is to use a cavitation system to reduce the contamination that enters the lake, at the same time that it transforms into gas methane and is reused in the form of energy.

CHRONOLOGY

August 31, 2016:
In search of saving the lake with modern technology, we signed an agreement with Oscar Amed Juarez, director of the Authority for the Sustainable Management of the Amatitlan Basin and Lake -AMSA-, in which we are authorized to carry out tests in the Lake and more importantly, the installation of our technology was established completely free, as a pilot project. The objective of this agreement was thatAMSA will perform water and sludge analysis at different points of the lake, including the area of our free pilot, weekly so that through This exercise will be demonstrated to the Guatemalan population and authorities, the actual cost of cleaning the Lake.

November 1, 2016:
We installed two cavitation machines in the Bahia Playa de Oro, in front of the "cleaning center" of AMSA, Despite the fact that the signed agreement also established that AMSA had to provide personnel and electrical equipment to facilitate installation; we were forced to buy 350 meters of TSJ cable, two voltage transformers to obtain three-phase power, flipones, as well as make a payment of Q100 to each AMSA employee who collaborated in the installation.

November 8, 2016:
One week after the installation of our pilot, the private laboratory LABIND carried out the sampling and analysis of the place and a result of 4.5ml / L of COD within our pilot's system, while the contamination concentration of the river is 700 ml / L, about 50 thousand kilograms of COD per day.

One month after installation, there were still no tests performed by AMSA, we send emails to Manuel Francisco Cano in charge of the Lake Control, Environmental Quality and Management Division of AMSA, and we made calls to the then director Amed Juarez requesting the analyzes, without receiving a response.
On several occasions we visited the pilot and found our machines turned off; the employees of AMSA and the guards never gave an explanation, in addition, the switches are in a cabin closed with chains and padlocks, so it was very difficult to turn the machines back on.

4 de febrero de 2017	APAGADAS
24 de febrero de 2017	APAGADAS
6 de marzo de 2017	APAGADAS
8 de marzo de 2017	APAGADAS
13 de marzo de 2017	APAGADAS
20 de marzo de 2017	APAGADAS
2 de abril de 2017	APAGADAS
9 de mayo de 29017	APAGADAS
20 de junio de 2017	APAGADAS
28 de julio de 2017 6 de agosto de 2017	APAGADAS

THE ANALYSIS

We have 12 analysis made in private laboratories, and despite the fact that the machines were not on all the time as agreed, the results are very good.
These analyzes were made possible by small activities with which we raised funds.

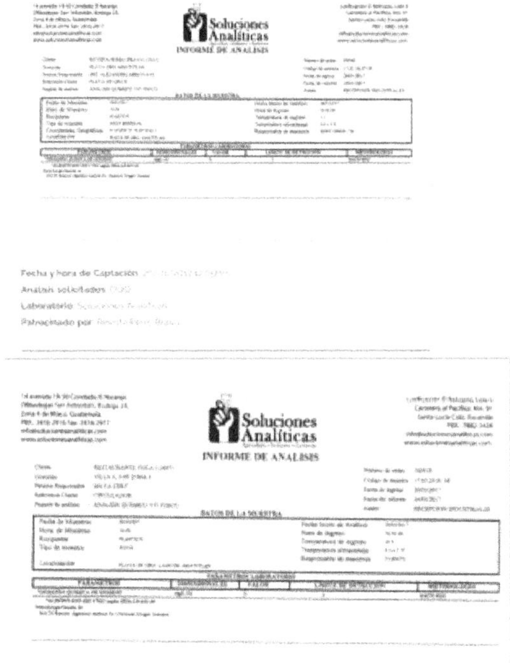

Soluciones Analíticas

INFORME DE ANALISIS

Fecha y hora de Captación: 26/01/2017
Análisis solicitados: DQO
Laboratorio: Soluciones Analíticas
Patrocinado por: Revista Perro Bravo

Soluciones Analíticas

INFORME DE ANALISIS

Soluciones Analíticas

INFORME DE ANALISIS

Fecha y hora de Captación: 26/01/2017
Análisis solicitados: DQO
Laboratorio: Soluciones Analíticas
Patrocinado por: Revista Perro Bravo

Fecha y hora de Captación: [illegible]

Análisis solicitados: DQO

Laboratorio: Soluciones Analíticas

Patrocinado por: Revista Perro Bravo

Fecha y hora de Captación: [illegible]

Análisis solicitados: DQO

Laboratorio: Soluciones Analíticas

Patrocinado por: Revista Perro Bravo

INFORME DE ANALISIS

Soluciones Analíticas

Fecha y hora de Captación: 26/01/2017 11:30hrs

Análisis solicitados: DQO

Laboratorio: Soluciones Analíticas

Patrocinado por: Pedro Bravo

INFORME DE ANALISIS

Soluciones Analíticas

Fecha y hora de Captación: 26/01/2017

Análisis solicitados: DQO

Laboratorio: Soluciones Analíticas

Patrocinado por: Revista Pedro Bravo

Soluciones Analíticas

INFORME DE ANALISIS

Fecha y hora de Captación:

Análisis solicitados:

Laboratorio: Soluciones Analíticas

Patrocinado por: Revista Perro Bravo

Soluciones Analíticas

INFORME DE ANALISIS

Fecha y hora de Captación:

Análisis solicitados:

Laboratorio: Soluciones Analíticas

Patrocinado por: Revista Perro Bravo

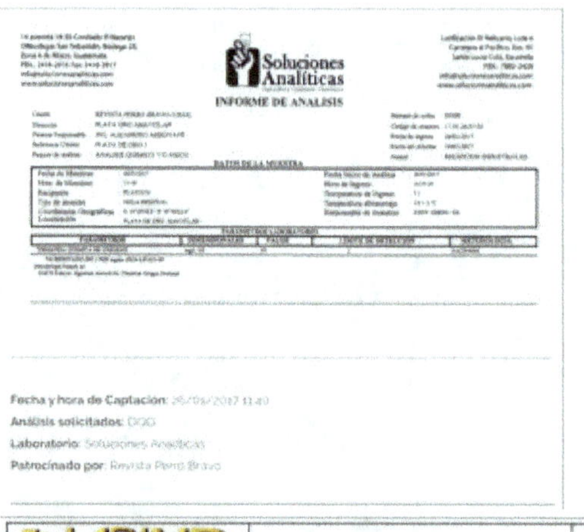

Fecha y hora de Captación: 26/05/2017 11:40

Análisis solicitados: DQO

Laboratorio: Soluciones Analíticas

Patrocinado por: Revista Perro Bravo

		Página 1 de 1

RESULTADO DE ANÁLISIS

Datos del Cliente

Atención a:	Sr. Alejandro Arroyave
Empresa:	CARTOTEC, S.A.
Dirección:	Lago de Amatitlán, Playa de Oro
Teléfono:	5692 1814
Correo electrónico:	Dato no proporcionado

Identificación de la Muestra

Tipo de muestra:	Agua de Lago
Lugar de captación:	Lago de Amatitlán, Playa de Oro
Fecha y hora de Captación:	08 de noviembre del 2016 11:30Hrs.
Captada por:	Personal Labind (Juan C. Gómez)
Identificación de la muestra:	SITUADO DENTRO DE LAS 2 MAQUINAS PLAYA DE ORO
Análisis solicitados:	Microbiología, DBO5, DQO Y OXIGENO DISUELTO

Datos de Ingreso al Laboratorio

No. de orden de servicio:	33,631	Hora de ingreso:	15:46 Horas
No. De Laboratorio:	52,467	Temp. de transporte °C.:	-
Fecha de ingreso:	08 de noviembre del 2016	Tipo de recipiente:	Plástico
Fecha de Inicio de análisis:	08 de noviembre del 2016		

Resultados de los Análisis Físicos y Químicos

Parámetro	Dimensionales	Resultado Laboratorio	Resultado Campo	Método de Referencia
Oxígeno Disuelto	mg/L	6.0	-	SMEWW-4500 OC
Demanda Química de Oxígeno (DQO)	mg/L	4.5	-	SQM²-14540
Demanda Bioquímica de Oxígeno (DBO5)	mg/L	3.2	-	SMEWW¹-5210 B

Resultados de los Exámenes Microbiológicos

Parámetro	Dimensionales	Resultado Laboratorio	Resultado Campo	Método de Referencia
Coliformes Totales	NMP/100mL	43	-	SMEWW¹-9221B
Coliformes Fecales	NMP/100mL	43	-	SMEWW¹-9221E
Escherichia coli	NMP/100mL	9	-	SMEWW¹-9223B

Método de muestreo SMEWW 1-1060 / 9060 A.

Aplica única y exclusivamente a las muestras captadas por personal de LABIND y/o personal capacitado por LABIND.

ND=No Detectable debajo del límite de detección.   * - * No efectuado   NE: No Especificado

1 Standard Methods For the Examination of Water and Wastewater, 21th ed. (SMEWW) American Water Works Association (AWWA), Water Environment Federation (WEF).
2Espectroquant Merck.   mg/L= miligramos por litro;ppm=partes por millón.   mL/L=mililitros por litro.   NMP: Número más Probable

Resultados válidos únicamente a la muestra analizada y tal como fue recibida en el laboratorio.

Los resultados de este informe no pueden ser reproducidos parcial o totalmente sin previa autorización del laboratorio.

El tiempo almacenamiento de registro: 4 años.

Transcrito por: Jessica Rodas.   Fecha de reporte: 16/11/2016

January 16, 2017:

On the contrary, Manuel Francisco Cano in charge of the
Lake Control, Environmental Quality and Management Division of
AMSA, sent by mail the supposed results of two analyzes that he
would have done in the area of our pilot, however, dates and
coordinates do not match our pilot project.
The pilot was installed in the Bahia Playa de Oro on November 1,
2016, but according to the document sent by Cano, the analyzes
were carried out on October 12 and 17, 2016, Y the coordinates
are far from being our pilot. According to the document sent by
Manuel Cano from AMSA, his analyzes were carried out in this
area:

But the pilot was installed in the Bahia Playa de Oro, while the coordinates used by Cano are from points outside the lake, according to the map, the search for these coordinates was confirmed by the Spanish ?Geologist Federico Mansilla.*

Analysis sent by Manuel, with coordinates that do not correspond to the point where the cavitators were.

INFORME DE RESULTADOS

INFORMACIÓN GENERAL

RESULTADOS DE ANÁLISIS

PARÁMETROS	Dimensional	Límite de detección	Resultado	Método
Demanda Química de Oxígeno (DQO)	mg/L	25	39	[illegible]
Demanda Bioquímica de Oxígeno (DBO)	mg/L	4	14	[illegible]

January 18, 2017:
Contacted us Manolo Ralda, neighbor and member of a
surveillance committee of Lake Amatitlán. Ralda offered all his
support, spoke4 with more members of his committee and
through them we managed to hold several conferences to inform
interested neighbors about the project.

February 1, 2017:
We contacted la la Regional School of Sanitary Engineering -
ERIS -, of the State University of Guatemala; With the support of
teachers, students and the vigilance committee, an experiment
was carried out under the supervision of students from the ERIS
and backed by AMSA.

After several months, emails, meetings, and requests, the
experiment was not carried out. (Attached you will find the
emails). During those negotiations, AMSA offered a
Geomembrane for the experiment. The geomembrane is placed
in sewage ponds to prevent contamination from seeping into the
ground and reaching drinking water sources; At the beginning, we
asked AMSA to carry out the pilot in a controlled lagoon with
geomembrane and flow meters, but the Lake authorities assured
that they did not have such equipment.

Manuel Cano wrote an email to our manufacturer in the United
States, requesting personal information on Douglas Lewis and
me, questioning the project's efforts to rescue the lake. The
agreement that AMSA signed established a confidentiality clause,
which was established since the agreement was not for purchase,
but for a free trial.

April 22, 2017:
We paid a visit to the pilot and found part of the equipment destroyed and also, several pieces were missing. No security guardAMSA He had reported it and when he asked, no one knew what had happened.

May 12, 2017:
We were invited to a meeting of Environment Commission - CIMA-, by Edgar Herbruger, inventor of the
National Secretary of Science and Technology - SENACYT-. At the meeting we presented our plan as a project and the CIMA members offered us support and gave us a guide to register the project before CONCYT-SENACYT.

June 7, 2017:
We present the project to the director of CONCYT- SENACYT, Oscar Cobar and offered to help with taking the pilot analysis through the San Carlos University.

July 3, 2017:
Amed Juarez and Manuel Cano arrived at the offices of SENACYT to tell director Oscar Cobar that our "machines are useless", this information was sent in an email by Edgar Herbruger and confirmed on July 17th by a representative of SENACYT at the CIMA meeting.

August 10, 2017:
Due to the constant sabotage of our pilot in the facilities of AMSA, We decided to remove our machines and take them to another lagoon. The Guatemalan company TOLEDO is looking for an economical and sustainable alternative to treat its water and they agreed to test our system.

August 14, 2017:
We announced to the Lake authorities that we had to take out our machines, the day we arrived at the facilities of Playa de Oro, the security personnel did not allow us access to the place. After talking on the phone with Marlon Alonzo, head of that area, we managed to enter.
For the first time, both Marlon Alonzo and the guards of the place, they were armed. Alonzo told us that we should sign a record stating that we were withdrawing our equipment. When we asked him to show us the record to read it carefully, Alonzo reacted aggressively; in a threatening tone he addressed us saying "NO FUCKING GRINGO IS GOING TO COME TO GIVE ME ORDERS, IF HE PUTS ME TO THE BRINCO, I WILL PUT A HIS BOOK AND I TAKE IT OUT OF HERE", reminding him that the machines were ours and not AMSA's, Alonzo replied "IF I SAY THAT THE MACHINES REMAIN, YOU CANNOT REMOVE THEM, YOU ARE IN PRIVATE PROPERTY", After talking on the phone with Amed Juarez and reminding him of the agreement and that the Lake is not private but public, Marlon Alonzo changed his attitude and offered us help to extract the machines from the water.

Collaboration agreement signed with AMSA

Wastewater Alchemy, Inc.
Douglas Jefferson Lewis

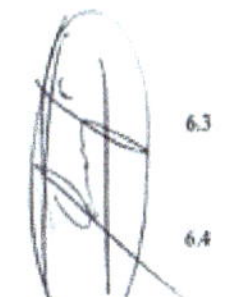

    la colocación de la máquina , los patrones de flujo, investigación, planes o especificaciones correspondientes.

b.   Nada en esta carta de entendimiento pretende o concede a una parte o a cualquier parte relacionada, ninguna licencia u otro derecho de cualquier naturaleza para utilizar cualquier información confidencial. Toda la información confidencial divulgada a cualquier parte seguirá siendo propiedad exclusiva de la parte reveladora de la información.

6.3   La Sección 6.1 no puede ser terminada unilateralmente por cualquiera de las partes, por ningún motivo y será vinculante para ambas partes indefinidamente. La terminación de esta carta de entendimiento no termina la sección 6.1 de este contrato.

6.4   Se acuerda expresamente que la identidad de cualquier persona o entidad y cualesquiera otros terceros (incluyendo, sin limitación, los proveedores, los clientes, las fuentes financieras, fabricantes y consultores) puestos a disposición por la parte reveladora, sea cualquier parte, con respecto al propósito de cualquier oportunidad de negocio relacionado, constituirán información confidencial y el receptor o cualquier grupo, empresa, entidad o individuo asociado, no deberá (sin el consentimiento previo por escrito de, o que ha suscrito un convenio de comisión con, la parte reveladora): iniciar directa o indirectamente, solicitar, negociar, contratar o entrar en cualquier transacción de negocios, convenios o empresas con esas terceras personas conocidas, identificadas o presentadas por la parte reveladora; o buscar pasar por encima, competir, evitar o eludir a la parte reveladora, desde o hacia cualquier oportunidad de negocio relacionada a la utilización de cualquier beneficio de la información confidencial.

6.5   Se acuerda expresamente que la "ingeniería inversa" de cualquiera de los diseños del sistema, incluyendo, sin limitación, las máquinas, la colocación de la máquina, el patrón de flujo y las cortinas, está expresamente prohibido.

6.6   El Receptor conviene que la ganancia financiera que haya realizado, o cualquier parte asociada, a partir de una violación de la cláusula 6.1, se llevará a depositar en beneficio de la parte reveladora y serán transferidos a una cuenta nominal de la Parte Reveladora y hasta entonces, la destacada cantidad generará los intereses a la tasa del   4 % anual por encima de la tasa LIBOR. Tal interés se devengará diariamente desde la fecha de vencimiento hasta el pago efectivo de la cantidad vencida, ya sea antes o después del juicio y el Receptor pagará el interés junto con la cantidad vencida.

6.7   La cláusula 6.5 no afecta la capacidad de la parte reveladora a demandar por daños también si los pactos en la cláusula 6.1 se violaran en modo alguno.

7 Carta de entendimiento

Este documento constituye el convenio completo y no hay representaciones orales o de otro tipo en relación con el objeto de la presente carta de entendimiento que sean vinculantes para ninguna de las partes. Todos los cambios a la carta de entendimiento deben hacerse por escrito, firmado por ambas partes.

8 Divisibilidad

Los términos de la carta de entendimiento son separables de tal manera que si cualquier término o disposición es declarada por un tribunal de jurisdicción competente como ilegal, nula o inejecutable, el resto de las disposiciones seguirán siendo válidas y ejecutables.

Wastewater Alchemy, inc.
Douglas Jefferson Lewis

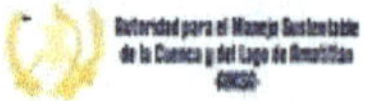

Convenio de préstamo de máquinas para prueba y propiedad intelectual entre **Wastewater Alchemy, inc. Douglas Jefferson Lewis** y la Autoridad para el Manejo Sustentable de la Cuenca de Lago de Amatitlán

En el municipio de Villa Nueva del departamento de Guatemala, el treinta y uno de agosto del dos mil dieciséis ubicados en la sede de la Autoridad para el Manejo Sustentable de la Cuenca de Lago de Amatitlán, ubicada en el kilómetro veintidós (22) carretera al pacífico ruta CA-9 Sur, compareciendo las personas siguientes: señor Douglas Jefferson Lewis, representante de la entidad **Wastewater Alchemy, inc.** Quien se identifica con pasaporte número 493050317, procedente de los Estados Unidos de Norteamérica, y por la otra parte el señor **Oscar Amed Juárez Sosa**, de cuarenta y un (41) años, casado, guatemalteco, ingeniero agrónomo, con domicilio en el departamento de Guatemala, quien se identifica con el documento personal de identificación número un mil seiscientos cuarenta, veinte mil seiscientos dieciséis cero ciento uno (1640 20616 0101) extendido por el Registro Nacional de las Personas –RENAP– de la República de Guatemala, actúo en mi calidad de Director Ejecutivo de la **Autoridad para el Manejo Sustentable de la Cuenca de Lago de Amatitlán**, que en adelante se podrá denominar AMSA, lo cual acredito con el Acuerdo Gubernativo de nombramiento número treinta y siete (37) de fecha uno (1) de febrero de dos mil dieciséis (2016) y certificación de acta de toma de posesión del cargo número cero seis guion dos mil dieciséis (06-2016), representaciones suficientes para llevar a cabo la firma de la presente carta de entendimiento de conformidad con lo siguiente:

EQUIPO

Máquina #1 número de serie LM15NA300866 con 3 caballos de fuerza (HP), trifásica, motor con número de serie ⟶ 2127702 .

Máquina #2 número de serie________________ con 3 caballos de fuerza (HP), trifásica, motor con número de serie ______________.

DECLARAN QUE

MIENTRAS, que AMSA es la institución con autoridad sobre las aguas y descargas en la cuenca del Lago Amatitlán; y

MIENTRAS, que AMSA desea eliminar algas y generalmente mejorar la calidad de agua en un área específica relativamente pequeña cerca de una playa pública; y

MIENTRAS, que Douglas Lewis está en el negocio de tratamiento de aguas negras y eliminación de lodos; y

MIENTRAS, que Douglas Lewis tiene un diseño para tratar el 100% del flujo del río Villalobos y también para tratar el lago y eliminar los lodos del lago; y

MIENTRAS, que por ahora, Douglas Lewis está de acuerdo con mejorar una sección del lago y eliminar los lodos en dicha área del lago; y

MIENTRAS que AMSA está de acuerdo para intentar ayudar a Douglas Lewis para implementar su plan para remediar el flujo completo del río Villalobos y mejorar la calidad del agua del lago de Amatitlán y eliminar lodos en el lago al mayor alcance posible; y

9   **Asignación**

Las partes no pueden ceder este Convenio (o prestar o arrendar o dar el equipo) a cualquier otra parte sin el consentimiento previo por escrito de las otras partes.

10   **Elección de Leyes / Jurisdicción**

Cualquier controversia o reclamo que surja de o esté relacionada con, esta carta de entendimiento, o el incumplimiento de la misma, se resolverá mediante arbitraje administrado por el Centro Internacional de Resolución de Disputas (CIRD), de convenio con sus reglas de arbitraje comercial y el juicio sobre el laudo dictado por el árbitro puede ser presentado en cualquier tribunal que tenga jurisdicción. Las reclamaciones serán atendidas por un solo árbitro. El lugar del arbitraje será la ciudad de Guatemala, Guatemala. El arbitraje se regirá por las leyes de Guatemala.

11   **Idioma**

El lenguaje en toda la carta de entendimiento será en todos los casos, simplemente construido de convenio con su justo significado y no estrictamente a favor o en contra de las Partes, y ambas partes están de convenio en que se utiliza el idioma español. No obstante, se acuerda que el arbitraje sería llevado a cabo en español.

12   **Honorarios y Costos**

El árbitro concederá a la parte ganadora, en su caso, según lo determinado por los árbitros, la totalidad de sus costos y honorarios. "Los costos y cargos " significan todos los gastos de pre - adjudicación razonable del arbitraje, incluyendo los árbitros, tasas, gastos administrativos, gastos de viaje, gastos de bolsillo tales como copias y teléfonos, los gastos judiciales, honorarios de testigos, y los honorarios de abogado. Las partes acuerdan que la falla o negativa de una parte a pagar su parte requerida de los depósitos de compensación al árbitro o los gastos administrativos constituirá una renuncia por esa parte a presentar pruebas o interrogar a los testigos. En tal caso, se requerirá a la otra parte para presentar pruebas y argumentos jurídicos que el árbitro pueda requerir para la realización de una retribución. Dicha renuncia no permite un juicio por defecto contra la parte que no paga en ausencia de evidencia presentada conforme a lo dispuesto anteriormente.

13   **Confidencialidad**

Salvo lo que se requiera por ley, ni una parte ni un árbitro pueden revelar la existencia, contenido o resultados de cualquier arbitraje de aquí en adelante sin el consentimiento previo por escrito de ambas partes.

Las personas abajo firmantes declaran y garantizan que están debidamente autorizados para ejecutar y entregar la presente carta de entendimiento en nombre de sí mismos y de su organización y que esta carta de entendimiento será obligatoria para cada parte de conformidad con sus términos, la cual queda contenida en cinco (5) hojas tamaño oficio, impresas únicamente en su anverso.

Ing. Oscar Amed Juárez-Sosa
Director Ejecutivo
Autoridad para el Manejo Sustentable de la
Cuenca y del Lago de Amatitlán

Douglas Jefferson Lewis
Wastewater Alchemy,

3.5 Los costos de muestreo y mapeo de profundidad de lodos estarán a cargo de AMSA.

3.6 Mantenimiento: se cambiará el aceite una vez por año usando aceite para caja de reductor Mobil SHC 630. Douglas Lewis llevará y cambiará el aceite bajo su propio costo.

3.7 Al momento de la firma de esta carta de entendimiento, se recibirá únicamente la máquina número uno y posteriormente se podrá instalar la máquina número dos y otros equipos.

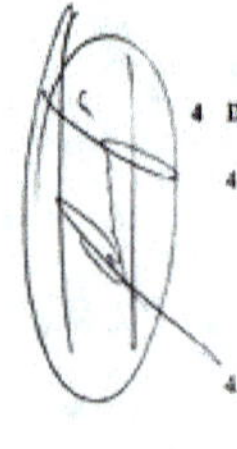

4 Duración de la carta de entendimiento

4.1 Exceptuando la cláusula 6.1, cualquier parte puede terminar el periodo de prueba en cualquier momento. Después de la terminación de cualquier parte por cualquier razón, AMSA pondrá a disposición para ser recogidas las máquinas de Douglas Lewis, en el lugar donde fueron instaladas, en 7 días empezando de la hora cuando la notificación sea enviada por correo electrónico.

4.2 Si el equipo no está disponible inmediatamente después del periodo de espera estipulado anteriormente, entonces AMSA se compromete a reponer el equipo por otro igual.

4.3 Si Douglas Lewis no recoge el equipo dentro del plazo de 7 días, el equipo se considera disponible (ver 4.2).

5 Condiciones del Equipo

AMSA acepta que regresará el equipo en las mismas condiciones en las que estaba cuando fue recibido, excepto el desgaste normal y ordinario. Si AMSA necesita reparar o reponer cualquier equipo durante el curso de su uso, dará aviso a Douglas Lewis para la reparación, asumiendo AMSA los gastos correspondientes, y estará obligado a regresar el equipo a Douglas Lewis al final del convenio.

6 Confidencialidad

6.1 Para facilitar la liberación de información entre las partes, esta carta de entendimiento establece las condiciones y obligaciones, en total, en torno a la revelación de una parte o toda la información confidencial relacionada en términos generales a; clientes, productos, propiedad intelectual, *know-how*, experiencia, métodos, patentes, productos, vendedores, proveedores y servicios de terceros.

6.2 Definiciones: Para el propósito de esta carta de entendimiento, los términos tendrán los significados siguientes:

   a. "Información Confidencial" significa cualquier información, sea implícita, explícita o inherente al sistema, escrita o verbal, que ha sido, o en adelante a esta fecha sea expuesta o revelada por alguna parte, o sus empleados, consultores y agentes, incluyendo toda información perteneciente o respecto a las tecnologías, diseños del sistema, miembros, proveedores, clientes y operaciones de las partes, incluyendo sin limitar a la generalidad de precedentes, toda la información técnica de cualquier naturaleza y todas las técnicas, invenciones, secretos comerciales, *know-how*, experiencia, descubrimientos, procesos, dibujos, diseños de las máquinas, cortinas,

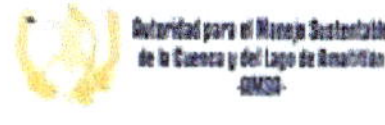

Wastewater Alchemy, inc.
Douglas Jefferson Lewis

MIENTRAS, que AMSA desea recibir en calidad de préstamo las máquinas y varios equipos específicos para la reducción de algas, con el objeto de ver los resultados de dichas máquinas con relación a la implementación del plan de Douglas Lewis para el flujo del río Villalobos, así como para las aguas y lodos del lago de Amatitlán; y

MIENTRAS, Douglas Jefferson Lewis desea entregar en calidad de préstamo las máquinas a AMSA, con el objeto que ellos evalúen la eficacia de las mencionadas máquinas, respecto a probar que el plan de Douglas Lewis para tratar el flujo del río, usando una porción del lago que está alrededor del río, es el plan más eficiente para tratar todo el flujo del río Villalobos.

AHORA, POR LO TANTO, en consideración de las cláusulas contenidas en este documento y para las consideraciones de otros productos y valores, la recepción y suficiencia de los cuales son reconocidos por los presentes, se acuerda y pacta mutuamente entre las partes para esta carta de entendimiento, lo siguiente:

1   **No hay Garantía de Aptitud.** Las Partes reconocen y aceptan que Wastewater Alchemy, Inc. no hace garantías o promesas respecto a los resultados de las máquinas en esta prueba en el Lago Amatitlán.

    1.1   AMSA acepta el equipo, en sus presentes condiciones, sin calificación.

2   **Convenio de Indemnidad.** Salvo causas de fuerza mayor, al mayor alcance permitido por la Ley, AMSA, indemnizará y mantendrá indemne a Wastewater Alchemy y a Douglas Lewis, de y contra cualquier reclamo, daños, y gastos, incluyendo pero no limitando a cuotas de abogados, que surjan del uso del equipo prestado y respecto al desempeño de sus operaciones o servicios, o cualquier acto, omisión, reclamo, o pérdida de cualquiera de sus empleados, agentes, voluntarios, participantes, invitados o cualquier otra parte de la que sean responsables, en conexión con el equipo, sin importar si ese reclamo, daño, pérdida o gasto, es causado en parte por una parte indemnizada en virtud del presente. Esta obligación no será interpretada para negar, abreviar o reducir otros derechos u obligaciones de indemnización que de otro modo existieran en ausencia de esta carta de entendimiento.

3   **Costos de esta prueba**

    3.1   Douglas Jefferson Lewis acuerda entregar en calidad de préstamo las máquinas sin costo alguno.

    3.2   AMSA acuerda pagar por todos los demás gastos para la prueba, incluyendo, mas no limitando a, instalación, incluyendo la apropiada conexión eléctrica, personal y el uso de un bote, remoción, costos operacionales, toma de muestras de DQO y cualquier dato que AMSA necesite para evaluar la eficiencia y eficacia de las mencionadas máquinas, así como los gastos del mapeo de la profundidad de los lodos.

    3.3   Fecha de inicio: las máquinas estarán disponibles a partir de la firma de este documento.

    3.4   Costos de operación: los costos operacionales estarán a cargo del propietario del sitio de esta prueba. Las máquinas de 3 HP consumirán alrededor de 2,500 kWh por mes, dependiendo del costo de la electricidad, podría llegar a ser alrededor de $150 dólares por máquina por mes.

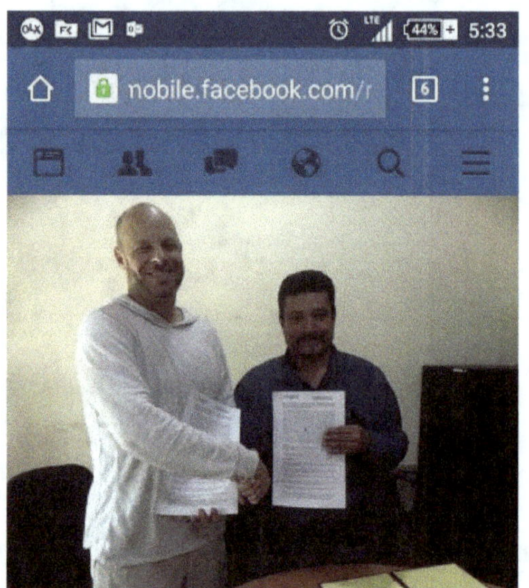

Revista Perro Bravo

Hoy AMSA y Wastewater Alchemy Inc. firmaron acuerdo de entendimiento para realizar pruebas gratuitas en el Lago Amatitlán con tecnología moderna, para reducir contaminación, algas y lodos, así como para transparentar el monitoreo de los mismos. #ReviveAmatitlán #CiudadanosPorElAgua

Timeline Photos · 2 hours ago ·

View Full Size · More Options

How would this test work?

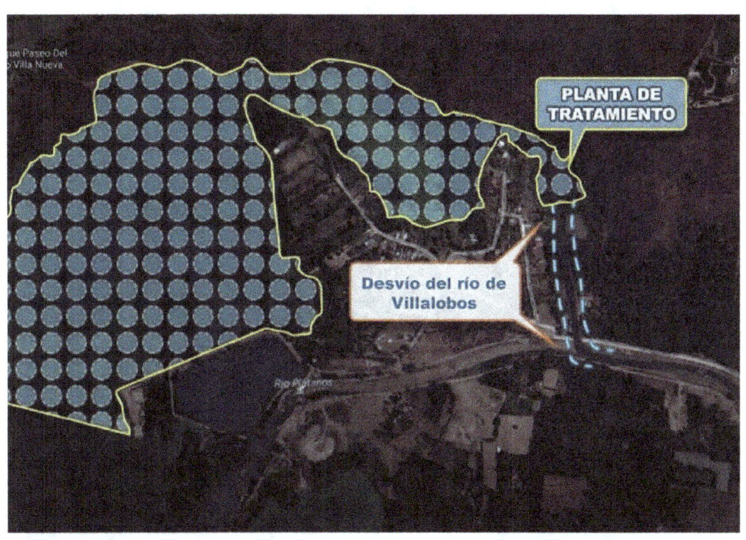

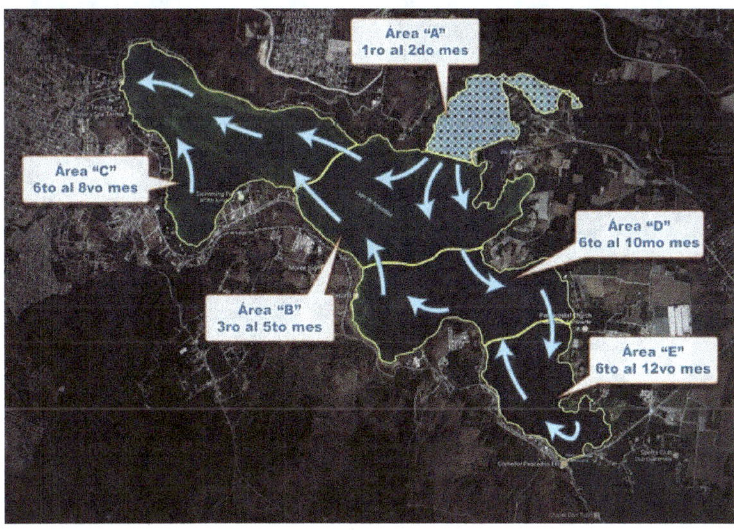

Laguna 2 (6 879 m2)
Laguna 1 (6 780 m2)
Línea de transmisión eléctrica
Google Earth

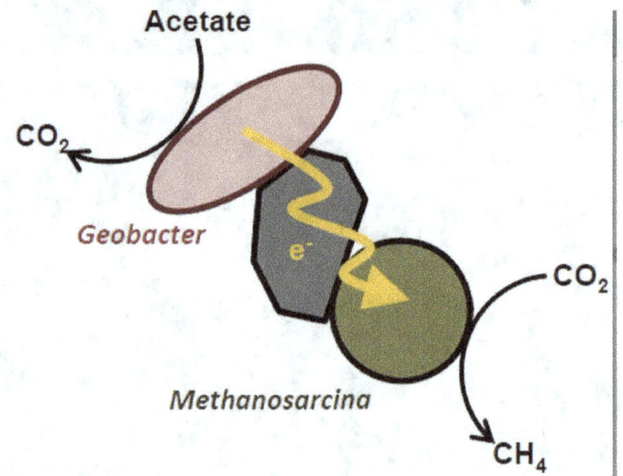

Acetate
CO2
Geobacter
e-
Methanosarcina
CO2
CH4

REVIVE! Amatitlan

Un costo aproximado en beneficio del análisis de Revive! Amatitlán es que por una inversión desde un par hasta varios millones de dólares de capital, la sociedad obtiene los siguientes beneficios:

- El agua del chorro podría ser potable (apta para beber).
- Los parques, casas y comunidades alrededor del lago podrían obtener fama y prestigio por su belleza y estilo de vida en el lago y los ingresos estatales remontarán como resultado en el incremento de impuestos de bienes raíces.
- Las casas flotantes, hoteles, restaurantes, bares y parques acuáticos florecerán alrededor del lago Amatitlán.
- Una nueva generación de criaderos libres de contaminación podría contener el lago con diversas especies de peces y camarones.
- Los lodos pueden ser transformados en agua y electricidad.
- CO_2 es secuestrado para formar gránulos de calcio de carbono, lo que contribuye a convertir el CO_2 adicional en gas metano, el cual produce electricidad.

El lago Amatitlán es fácil y barato de revivir.

Para revivir el lago Amatitlán, el flujo del río Villalobos debe ser tratado continuamente, el agua del lago debe ser remediada y el lodo, eliminado.

En un pequeño piloto en curso, en el lago, cerca de playa oro, el agua está entre 75% y 93% más limpia después de solo siete días y el lago en ese área es dos meses más profundo después de sólo 1 mes. Esto demuestra cómo remediar el agua y eliminar lodos acumulados por décadas.

Antes (datos provistos por AMSA)		Después 7 días de amansar la prueba (datos provistos por LABIND)
Fecha	DQO mg/L	DQO mg/L
1/11/16	25.2	
4/12/16	27	
	20.5	
6/1/16	50	
	30	
8/22/16	73	
	63	
	37	
11/8/16		4.6

Los propósitos del piloto es ver y publicar el costo real de capital y de operaciones para revivir el lago Amatitlán. Una vez se hayan tomando suficientes análisis (por terceras partes), esperamos que los datos indiquen que un capital total de alrededor de+/- dos millones USD (Q14,943,000 aprox.) es suficiente para remediar el 100% del flujo de río Villalobos, para eliminar rápidamente los lodos dentro del sistema de

Relevant biochemical pathways to eliminate sludge:

- The syntophic consortia primarily *Geobacter* species & *methanosaeta* species exchange electrons via a **Direct Interspecies Electron Transfer**:

- $2_e^- + 2H^+ \rightarrow H_2$ and the H_2 serves as the electron donor for methane production:

- $4H_2 + CO_2 \rightarrow CH_4 + 2CO_2$

- $2CH_3COOH \rightarrow 2CH_4 + 2CO_2$

- $CO_2 + 8_e^- + 8H^+ \rightarrow CH_4 + 2H_2O$

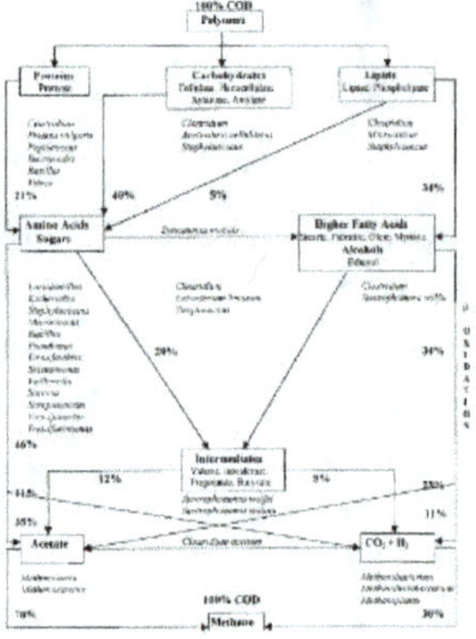

ig 24.2 Carbon flow to methane in anaerobic digesters with the microorganisms responsible for each step. Adapted from Gujer and Zehnder, 1983

SELECTOR SYSTEM

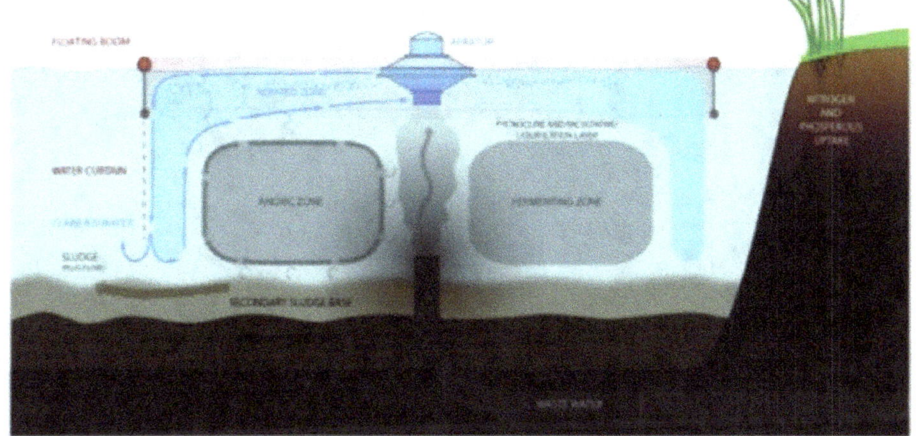

Success Stories

"Clear Lake", California.

"REPSA", Peten, Guatemala.

"Nutriagaves", Jalisco, México.

"Grupo SRS" Puebla, México

"Nutriagaves", Jalisco, México.

"Travellers Rum", Belice.

"Granja del Toro", Ciudad Guzmán, Jalisco, Mexico.

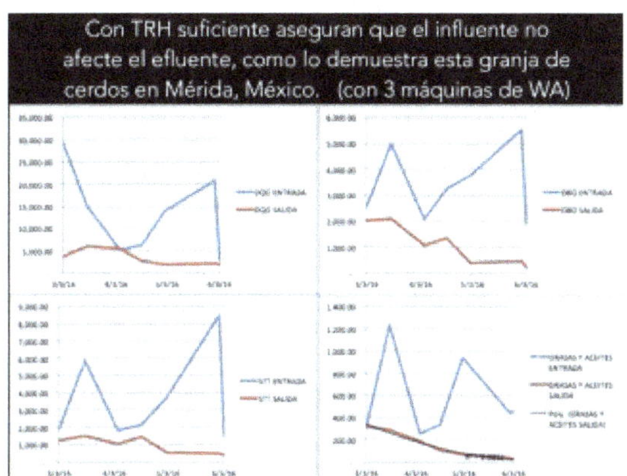
Con TRH suficiente aseguran que el influente no afecte el efluente, como lo demuestra esta granja de cerdos en Mérida, México. (con 3 máquinas de WA)

ERIS EXPERIMENT MAIL:

Desde: Eduardo Villagrán <eduardo.villagran@gmail.com>
Sent: Thursday, February 2, 2017 10:19 AM
To: 'Alvaro Hurtado '; 'alhurt56'; 'Asesoria Manuel Basterrechea'; 'Antonio Guirola'; 'Luis Flores'; 'Gabriel Biguria'; 'Manolo Ralda'; 'Ricardo Erales C.'; 'Silvia de Erales'; 'JUAN BOTRAN'
Cc: 'Lake Amatitlán Committee '
Subject: Meeting on cavitation technology

Hello dears,

On Tuesday afternoon, we met with Douglas Lewis, Daniela Schottler and Alejandro Arroyave to advance the subject of the analysis of this technology.

to.

Manuel Basterrechea is making arrangements for the Regional School of Sanitary Engineering - ERIS - to assign a final year student to the evaluation of the equipment that REVIVE has installed in Playa de Oro. This will include experimental design, sampling and analysis. lysis, evaluation and recommendations. The friends of REVIVE expressed their satisfaction with the implementation of this approach and will be meeting with one of the ERIS teachers this week.

REVIVE has installed some equipment in Guatemala and others are known in Mexico. They were asked to make a joint evaluation of their performance. Doug Lewis agreed to contact the

b.

CD

owners and organize the evaluation visits, in which Manuel and a server would participate, in principle; welcome others.

It was agreed to continue developing the White Report, which will nevertheless depend on the results obtained in numbers 1 and 2.

Manuel Ralda accompanied those from REVIVE on a visit yesterday, in order to fine-tune the location of the equipment and the experimental design, including the redirection of waters from the Villalobos River to the cavitators.

We continue to advance on other fronts. Greetings Eduardo
Desde: Eduardo Villagrán <eduardo.villagran@gmail.com>
Sent: Tuesday, January 31, 2017 2:49 PM
To: 'Doug Lewis'; 'Manolo Ralda'; 'Alejandro Arroyave'; 'Manuel
Basterrechea Advisory'DC:

 'Daniela Alvarez Schottler'; reviveamatitlan@gmail.com Subject:
White report
Dear All,
I enclose a possible index for the White Report that I propose to
carry out to evaluate the hydrodynamic cavitation technology in
Amatitlán.
We can discuss it during our meeting. Greetings Eduardo

____

Hi all.
Yesterday I met with Daniela Schottler and Douglas Lewis,
developers of the cavitation project. Several comments to share
with you.
- They invested and continue to invest of their own money to
install two diggers in the Playa de Oro area and pay for the water
analysis despite having signed an agreement with AMSA
according to which it would carry out the analysis. Attached aerial
photo and very indicative results, nothing robust.
- They have little experience in project development and when
they saw that AMSA did not comply with the agreement, they got
upset, without understanding how bureaucracies work in
Guatemala; This has soured the relationship between them and
led to mutual recriminations.
- Technology offers good potential at a lower cost than others; I
copy below an abstract that summarizes it and a presentation of
how it works.

- Taking advantage of what they already have installed, their enthusiasm and their commitment to the lake and the good disposition of some of

 we are going to do a White paper summarizing its potential for application to the Amatitlán problem.
- East White paper will include a protocol for the analysis of the pilot plan that they are carrying out including the justification of the technology based on its theoretical aspects and especially the experience in other parts, the design for the statistical sampling of the area at different depths, the analysis of samples to see the behavior of COD, P and N, residence times and capital and operating costs, among other things.
- With this plan, support in the analysis can be arranged either with AMSA or ERIS or with another public or private group.
- Throughout Manuel B. and I will advise Doug and Daniela to be more systematic in their work and Manuel R. to market themselves better.
- They discussed the possibility of treating the East side first, installing diggers where it is most efficient.
For all the above, I do not believe that a meeting is timely yet, members of the Committee and Monica, until we have the White Paper. Otherwise there is a risk that the enthusiasm and amateurism of the developers will detract from the credibility of the technology.
Abstract:
"The use of acoustic cavitation for water and wastewater treatment (cleaning) is a well known procedure. Yet, the use of hydrodynamic cavitation as a sole technique or in combination with other techniques such as ultrasound has only recently been suggested and employed. In the first part of this paper a general overview of techniques that employ hydrodynamic cavitation for cleaning of water and wastewater is presented. In the second part

of the paper the focus is on our own most recent work using hydrodynamic cavitation for removal of pharmaceuticals (clofibric

 acid, ibuprofen, ketoprofen, naproxen, diclofenac, carbamazepine), toxic cyanobacteria (Microcystis aeruginosa), green microalgae (Chlorella vulgaris), bacteria (Legionella pneumophila) and viruses (Rotavirus) from water and wastewater. As will be shown, hydrodynamic cavitation, like acoustic, can manifest itself in many different forms each having its own distinctive properties and mechanisms. This was until now neglected, which eventually led to poor performance of the technique. We will show that a different type of hydrodynamic cavitation (different removal mechanism) is required for successful removal of different pollutants. The path to use hydrodynamic cavitation as a routine water cleaning method is still long, but recent results have already shown great potential for optimization, which could lead to a low energy tool for water and wastewater cleaning. " -http://www.sciencedirect.com/science/ article / pii / S1350417715300 535
Use of hydrodynamic cavitation in (waste) water treatment ... www.sciencedirect.com
The use of acoustic cavitation for water and wastewater treatment (cleaning) is a well known procedure. Yet, the use of hydrodynamic cavitation as a sole technique or ...
Presentation
This PowerPoint summarizes the principles of the technology and its applications. In the end it is a bit general and the example you use is not from sewage treatment but from industrial sewage but it gives a good idea of how it works.https://prezi.com/ d1g7g5ojwrbr / hydrodynamic-cavitation-and- waste-water- treatment /
Hydrodynamic Cavitation and Waste water

 treatment - Prezi prezi.com

Contents: Why Hydrodynamic Cavitation ... Hydrodynamic
Cavitation and reactors -a novel technique for waste water
treatment Utsab Banerjee ME13M046
Costs
Doug talks about Q5 million to treat the Villalobos River
permanently which seems too low to me. Still, if it were 10
times higher it would still be cheaper than the alternatives, so this
technology and its application to the lake should be further
studied.
We continue to work on all other fronts. Greetings and good
weekend to all.
Edward
Dear Eduardo,
thank you for sending the report!
one question, "Although the Villalobos river receives the pollutant
load of all the rivers that make up its basin, the latter presents the
lowest pollutant load values (COD: 44,150 Kg / day and BOD:
16,623 Kg / day)
- Source: Control, Environmental Quality and Management of
Lagos, 2016. "
according the vp, this was reduced by 40% in 2017, correct? i
have not yet found that reduction reflected this document. id love
to get a copy of the updated results and copies of the background
records of flow and COD concentrations whenever that would be
convenient.
thanks!
On Mar 3, 2017, at 11:56 AM, Eduardo Villagrán
<eduardo.villagran@gmail.com> wrote:
Good morning to everybody.
I spoke with Amed and he says that, indeed, he already had his
surveyor scheduled for other activities but that on Monday or
Tuesday he sends him to measure the lagoon so that we can do
the calculations and install the equipment. This pace of work is

normal in a State organization and we will have to take it into account.

I also share with Doug and Daniela and Manolo the excellent report that Manuel Cano sent regarding the contamination of the rivers of the Basin; the dimension in Table 10 is MPN / 100 ml, or the most probable number per 100 milliliters.
With that we would be ready to start next week. Greetings and good weekend, Eduardo
Of: Doug Lewis [mailto: dougbamboolewis@gmail.com]
Sent on: Wednesday, March 01, 2017 09:10 pm
To: Eduardo Villagrán
DC: Consulting Manuel Basterrechea; Alejandro Arroyave; Alvaro Hurtado; Alvaro Hurtado; Antonio Guirola; Daniela Alvarez Schottler; Manolo Ralda; Relive Amatitlán
Matter: Re: Meeting with Amed Juárez
it would be my pleasure to pay for the pipe. Thank you!
On Mar 1, 2017, at 8:43 PM, Eduardo Villagrán

-

-

-

-

<eduardo.villagran@gmail.com> wrote: Dear Doug and Manuel,
I think we must do our best with what AMSA is offering, which is:
Working at the small lagoon
Raising the borders, to get a depth that Doug considers will allow the equipment to work in a representative manner

Injecting Villalobos river water through a pipe; Amed suggested two inches in diameter, that can change based on desirable flow for optimum results
Taking flow and water quality samples at the intake and the outflow for a representative time period to be suggested by Doug

The idea is to show whether there are significant water quality improvement results. They may not be optimal at this point, just good enough to convince AMSA to continue on to a larger test and pilot project.

Is it possible for you to come up with the pipe, Doug? Look forward to the statistical comparisons! Edward

Of: Consultancy Manuel Basterrechea [mailto: asebaste@gmail.com]

Sent on: Wednesday, March 01, 2017 06:13 pm

To: Doug lewis

DC: Eduardo Villagrán; Alejandro Arroyave; Alvaro Hurtado; Alvaro Hurtado; Antonio Guirola; Daniela Alvarez Schottler; Manolo Ralda; Relive Amatitlán

Matter: Re: Meeting with Amed Juárez

Doug, I recommend that we do what AMSA proposes in order to show that the selector and circulator works. That way AMSA will be participating in the research. Then we can develop a long term pilot research. AMSA has its own projects, and is planning to buy land to do so. Therefore, we must move fast.

Greetings

Manuel

2 0 1 7 - 0 3 - 0 1 1 7: 4 1 GMT- 0 6: 0 0 D oug L ewis < dougbamboolewis@gmail.com>:

the issue with the pond visa vi geomembrana, according to

amsa, was or is that the pond fills up with water, it cannot be drained.

the HRT of the test could be 30 days.

i believe that if the river is moved back to one of my recommended entrance point, that the HRT of the system will be many months or more.

I would like to see a long term pilot, either this one or the actual installation or another, where we slowly change the HRT in order to see which HRT is the best combination of the lowest cost per kg. of COD coupled with results that most noticeably change the lake between the system and the exit river.

That is, if the water were too clean and did not have archaea, facultative bacteria, anaerobic bacerteria and caco3 nuclei the lake will not clean itself. so a system HRT of maybe 25 days is probably going to be the best.

of course we can do without a control pond. the lake has years of HRT and the DQO ranges from 40-70, according to amsa.

On Mar 1, 2017, at 11:23 AM, Asesoria Manuel Basterrechea < asebaste@gmail.com> wrote:

Doug, I think that we can do without a control pound. We can use the AMSA geomembrane to avoid the infiltration from outside.

What detention time do you recommend for the pound, in order to estimate the inflow coming from Río Villalobos?

On Wed, Mar 1 from 2017 at 10:23 a.m., Eduardo Villagrán < eduardo.villagran@gmail.com> wrote:

One thing that bothers me about the lagoon is that we won't be able to set up the witness pond without treatment, for comparison and control. What do you think, Manuel?

On a lighter note last night I had dinner at Mercado 24 and was pleased to find a painting of the Blue Frog and hear from the owner how they are cooperating with REVIVE.

Edward

Of: Doug Lewis [mailto:dougbamboolewis@gmail.com]

Sent on: Tuesday, February 28, 2017 05:41 pm

To: Eduardo Villagrán

DC: Daniela Alvarez Schottler; Manolo Ralda; Consulting Manuel Basterrechea; Alejandro Arroyave; Revive Amatitlán; Alvaro Hurtado; Alvaro Hurtado; Antonio Guirola

Matter: Re: Meeting with Amed Juárez

a great advantage of the lagoon that is on their property is that it will not be affected by rain, especially if it is lined. On Feb 28, 2017, at 5:40 PM, Eduardo Villagran <

eduardo.villagran@gmail.com> wrote:
I think that's right, Doug. Manuel can confirm that this is the
laguneta. The points you mention are good ones and the possible
solution for the infiltration too; I think Amed has plastic membrane
and I don't see the reason not to use it, do you Manuel? We did
discuss the depth but Amed is willing to raise the border a meter
or so; again, technical comments welcome.
Now that we are all back at the table let's move forward before
the rainy season begins.
Till later, Eduardo

 On February 28, 2017, 16:09, Doug Lewi s <
dougbamboolewis@gmail.com> wrote: Thanks Eduardo and
Manuel !!
just to make sure that i understand, are we talking about this
lagoon on the amsa property?
if so, i am satisfied with that location. lets move forward. we will
need a flow meter that measures the total flow.
The reasons that it was turned down in the past were: • from
amsa side, they said that they
needed an environmental permit. • from my side, because it is
connected to the water table we
cannot know the HRT.
• because contaminated water is
infiltrating the lagoon, we cannot know the quantity of
concentrations entering the system.
• Anotherrealityisthatitisnotdeepandsowillnotmodelthe results of
the actual project. I forgot how deep AMSA said that it is. but, it
needs to be deep enough that algae will not be able to
photosynthesis when they are sunk.
of course the ideal solution would be to line it with geomembrane.
amsa told me that this is impossible. if anybody thinks otherwise,
please let me know.
thanks!

<PastedGraphic-12.png>
On Feb 28, 2017, at 4:35 PM, Eduardo Villagran

 <eduardo.villagran@gmail.com> wrote: Hello,
Today we meet with him Manuel and a server. He said that the earthmoving machinery is from the sandboxes and that they collaborate with him sometimes. To fill in the two gaps on the chosen site, you would have to hire them.
He said that there is another lagoon near the recreational area and that AMSA could divert water from Villalobos directly to it. All it would take is someone, maybe Doug, to run the 100 meters of two-inch plastic tubing to make the connection; AMSA would put the rest. The two Blue Frogs could be installed there, measuring and sampling the inlet and outlet of the water.
Manuel agreed, they agreed to do the bathymetry of that little lagoon and we to talk about it with Quique and Félix. Otherwise, he was willing to collaborate with the evaluation as much as possible. I didn't hear that he stayed on a specific schedule but Amed appointed the deputy director, Carolina, to follow up, without excluding himself from continuing on the play.
We are then on the way to a technical evaluation of the Blue Toads, because although the experimental design is modified, he and the AMSA are already involved; it will be up to the technicians and Doug, as to what the team can do, to finalize the research protocol.
Greetings, Edward
Of: Manuel Cano [mailto: manuelfcano@gmail.com] Sent on: Thursday, 20 of

 April 2017 02:04 pm
To: Consulting Manuel Basterrechea
DC: Felix Aguilar; Carol Tobar; Carolina Tobar; AMSA Director; Eduardo Villagrán; Enrique Godinez
Matter: Re: Protocol

I comment that currently the San Agustín plant does not have electricity, so the treatment plant would be the
Cerra, located in Villa Canales. It does not have electricity but at no more than 600 m we have 480 and 220 energy where energy could be taken.
If that's okay with you, we can meet tomorrow, just set the time.
Kind regards.
On April 20, 2017, 12:52 p.m., Asesoria Manuel Basterrechea < asebaste@gmail.com> wrote:
Sure, it could be early in the morning.
Greetings
On Thu, Apr 20 from 2017 at 12:46 p.m., Felix Aguilar < iagcons@gmail.com> wrote:
Dear, I agree with what Manual proposes, let's just coordinate a visit to the area as soon as possible. I will speak with Enrique this afternoon at the University to suggest a date, although I tentatively think it could be Monday, I don't know how they see it.
On April 20, 2017, 10:03, Asesoria Manuel Basterrechea < asebaste@gmail.com> wrote:
Dear, good morning.
According to Manuel's proposal, because the purpose is to evaluate the treatment efficiency of the equipment. When could we go to visit the lagoons? Please send the dimensions of the gaps and their retention time.

Greetings
Manuel
T he April 1 9 2 0 1 7, 2 2: 0 7, M anuel C anus < manuelfcano@gmail.com> wrote:
Thank you dear Doctor,
As we discussed today in the morning, in order to work on the implementation of the geomembrane in the artificial lagoon of Playa de Oro, it is necessary to have a company that carries out the welding of the same, to cover the dimensions of the lagoon

and avoid the infiltration and contamination of the sub-surface water with waters from the Villalobos river that could affect the community. This process will take time depending on the area that we want to waterproof, without taking into account the cost that it represents. However, if what we want to verify with this equipment is the reduction of sludge through cavitation processes that this company justifies, I consider it convenient to do it in one of the anaerobic lagoons that already have this wastewater.
I propose that this option be evaluated if what is desired is to gain time prior to the rainy season that may affect the results. At the same time, the laboratory has tubes for collecting wastewater sludge (sewage tube samplers) to support the equipment for taking samples.
If it is decided to empty the sludge lagoon and fill it with wastewater, it must be taken into account that these processes provide only 10% of sludge, because the rest of the digestion goes through methanogenesis, so we should have two lagoons To compare results, otherwise we could not define that the absence of sludge is due to the installed equipment. Similarly, if we wish to evaluate the reduction in pollutant load, a reduction is already expected as it is found in a closed system saturated with methanogenic bacteria and the analysis

 it would be more focused on debugging times. Therefore and in my opinion, it will be better to carry out the tests in two lagoons (eg Lagunas de la cerra or San Agustín) one with treatment and the other without treatment to be able to compare results and percentage of effectiveness.
I consider it convenient that both the advisor and the student evaluate this option, in order to broaden the criteria for the implementation of the team effectiveness study.
Sincerely, Manuel Cano
April 19, 2017, 15:59, Asesoria Manuel Basterrechea < asebaste@gmail.com> wrote:

Manuel good afternoon.
I copy this email to ERIS Professor Felix Aguilar and to the professional who will do his special study Enrique Godínez, of the protocol to follow. It is urgent to start as soon as possible to avoid that the beginning of the rainy season could affect the operation of the lagoon (groundwater entry through the bottom).
The purpose is to evaluate the wastewater treatment efficiency of the equipment. Enrique would take water samples 2 times a week for at least 6 weeks and do the analyzes in the RIS / Faculty of Engineering laboratory.
It is necessary for AMSA to empty the lagoon, place the geomembrane and fill the lagoon; If the lagoon is shallow, it will be necessary to build a fence around it to reach more than 2.5 meters.
Greetings
Manuel --

 Lic. Manuel Francisco Cano Tel .: 47665365
--
Ing. Felix Aguilar
--
Lic. Manuel Francisco Cano Tel .: 47665365
EMAILS BETWEEN AMSAY REVIVE AMATITLÁN
Good afternoon Doug, I hereby attach laboratory results of the equipment installed 1 meter away and 100 m away.
It is worth mentioning that the results that I sent last year were recorded in the laboratory as aerators but they refer to the equipment that your company represents.
Atte,
--
Lic. Manuel Francisco Cano

Doug attached the info.
WWTP San Agustín, Boca del Monte, Villa Canales, and
summary of areas. Areas: Anaerobic lagoon 1: 3200 m2
> Anaerobic lagoon 2: 3200 m2
> Optional lagoon 1: 8750 m2> Optional lagoon 2: 7,000 m2
Greetings ...
Doug, I am attaching coordinates of the plant 14.527534,
-90.524142

--

Lic. Manuel Francisco Cano Tel .: 40952232 Dear,
thank you for your time today.

 Here is the proposal for a test by amsa. The idea is to start today
and by using the results of this test in a few months we are going
for a bigger test and so on.
Tomorrow we go to San Agustin at 12 I think.
Thank you
doug
5955 7814
http://www.wastewateralchemy.com

Desde: Manuel Cano <manuelfcano@gmail.com> Subject: Re:
Laboratory Results Date:
October 10, 2016 at 1:21:58 PM CST
To: Doug Lewis <dougbamboolewis@gmail.com> DC: AMSA
Director <oamedjuarez@hotmail.com>
http ps: / / ma il - att achmen t. goog l euse r with t in t. com / att
achmen t /. . .OmAERgx15z_b2KdTBd20KrxQYUf9-
HXj630kCsbz5mLKZ6R7g 01/04/2020, 12W39 Page 27 of 41
Good afternoon Doug,
Apologies in advance for replying a bit late.
Based on the sampling and analysis of water and sludge on the
public beach, I do not know the methodology that is intended to

be used to evaluate the operation of the equipment. Therefore, I will be grateful to you for transferring the monitoring plan and type of analysis to be carried out to include it within our planning, with the intention of avoiding errors and a misinterpretation of the operation of the equipment due to variables unrelated to its operation and scope, such as Example: aeration of nearby equipment with higher power, O2 hypersaturation of the epilimnion, low retention due to the effect of the Michatoya River. The idea is that we can generate the information without being affected by a methodology decision proposed by the laboratory unit that is not the appropriate one.

Sincerely, Manuel Cano

October 6, 2016, 1:58 PM, Doug Lewis <dougbamboolewis@gmail.com> wrote: Dear Manuel, eat these?

two questions. do you have the results for the other 2 samples? I want because the HRT is 4 days and I want to see what the percentage can be reduced with 4 days of HRT (residence). For helping design the size of the curtains in ematittlan this or next month.

And have you already taken water samples and have you measured the depth of sludge by our installation in the public beach? Thank you, Doug

On Jul 8, 2016, at 11:18 AM, Manuel Cano <manuelfcano@gmail.com> wrote: Dear Doug, I am hereby sending you lab results.

Sincerely,

--

Lic. Manuel Francisco Cano Tel .: 47665365 <rtdo COD 0143016.pdf>

--

Lic. Manuel Francisco Cano
Tel .: 47665365

Good Manuel, we understand that so far no analysis has been carried out, we have scheduled a sampling for Tuesday at 10:39 at next gold beach by a private laboratory. I hereby request that you provide us with the historical data of the lake area in Playa Oro. All the information you have available will be of use to us. Thanks a lot! Doug

 Use whatsapp 415 377 5043 Sent from my iPhone
Begin forwarded message:
Desde: Manuel Cano <manuelfcano @ gmai l.com> Subject: Methodology for teams Date:
January 16, 2017 at 3:42:09 PM CST
To: Doug Lewis <dougbamboolewis@gmail.com>, AMSA Director <oamedjuarez@hotmail.com>
DC: ctobar@amsa.gob.gt
Good afternoon dear Doug,
By means of this sending information requested from Lake Amatitlán and on Wednesday I hope to transfer the results of the COD and BOD analysis laboratory carried out in an area close to the equipment that you offer.
Regarding the definition of methodologies that may be useful to measure the efficiency of the equipment that Wastewater Alchemy offers, I consider that it is necessary to define it together, through your technical team and technical staff from AMSA and collaborators, for a methodology endorsed by both.
However, analyzing the way of proposing the methodology we would need complementary information based on:
• Distance range that must exist between the sludge and digging teams
• Installation way and curtains design to avoid the subsurface flow of streams
• Minimum residence times that the

 water in contact with the equipment

• Radius of action of the equipment for installation •
Bioaugmentation effect that may occur due to
sludge movement
On the other hand, I would appreciate transferring information on
the technical specifications of the equipment and operating
method in open water bodies, since the hydrodynamic cavitation
processes that I found are associated with wastewater. This in
order to avoid a bad experimental design that results in a
misinterpretation and reliability of the information obtained.
Sincerely,

--

Lic. Manuel Francisco Cano Tel .: 47665365
Good afternoon dear Manuel,
Below I answer some of your questions and attach a document
with the scientific explanation of what our technology does.
We wait until today Thursday to obtain the laboratory results of
the COD analyzes carried out in the area near the installed
cavitation machines, we understand that it may take more time so
I proceed to comment on the information sent so far, which
continues to be scarce.
- As we can see with the only two measurements sent in relation
to the aerators, it is that these do remove but generate more
sludge, hence a concentration of 63 mg / L at 1 meter distance
and 39 mg / L at 100 meters away. This does not happen with our
CAVITATION machines, precisely because they remove sludge. If
the sludge were moving from one side to the other, it would be
shown in the concentration of contamination in the water, that is,
our COD measurement, in the middle of the machines, between
15 and 10 meters away from the equipment, would be much
higher than 4.5 mg / L.
- Our technology removes sludge by transforming that carbon
material through the installation of an ecosystem in which archaea
predominates. As you will understand in the attached document,
we want the archaea to dominate the system in such a way that

the contamination is translated into pure water, methane and a bottom made up of CaCo3 granules. That is why it is very important not only to measure the depth of the sludge, which will be greatly reduced, but also the mapping of sludge should include analysis of the chemical composition of the bottom, because there we will find that it has changed and, therefore, behaves differently.
- We agree with the methodology that you apply to evaluate the other water treatment projects, but we propose that the reduction of COD and the elimination of sludge be the parameters with which any other proposed treatment is compared. As you can see in the results sent to us, there is no point that even comes close to the reduction evidenced two weeks after installing the CAVITATING machines. We can spend the whole year discussing study methodologies, but we must focus on what is already happening and do everything possible to validate it, for you and so will universities and private laboratories, so that we have all the scientific evidence. available to justify any public investment to clean up the lake.

- You have in your hands, and it is your duty, to collaborate and facilitate the necessary analysis to make transparent what is happening with this pilot, who has shown results that have never been recorded in the history of AMSA. Let's avoid getting complicated and let's be practical in approaching this pilot in order to objectively evaluate the various water treatment projects for Lake Amatitlán. We insist: the reduction of COD and the elimination of sludge must be the parameters that determine the quality of the results of this technology, and compared to any other.
We are sure that after reading the attached document, you will be able to understand more easily why the following answers:
- There is no range that "should" exist between sludge and digging equipment. They work whatever that distance.

- The curtains have the purpose of establishing a HRT and maintaining a flow in order to identify the reduction cost per kg of COD. These will be installed from the surface to more than 1 meter deep, joined and without open spaces. No surface or subsurface current will influence that area.
- We do not think of a minimum HRT, the teams do their work with any HRT, we think rather around obtaining the maximum possible HRT because that implies a lower cost per kg reduced and that is in the interest of taxpayers . Nobody wants to spend more taxes on more expensive options. We should think around as much HRT as possible to clean more.
http ps: / / ma il - att achmen t. goog l euse r with t in t. com / att achmen t /. . .OmAERgx15z_b2KdTBd20KrxQYUf9-HXj630kCsbz5mLKZ6R7g 01/04/2020, 12W39 Page 30 of 41
- The radius of action of the equipment is very extensive since sine waves are generated that go out in all directions. They must consider that the radius of action where they are installed reaches up to the shores that surround the area.
- We repeat: there is no movement of sludge, there is elimination and transformation.
In conclusion, we agree on the consensus reached with AMSA in our last meeting, for taking samples from 10, 20, 40, 50, 100, 200+ of the machines, towards at least 8 cardinal orientations, to analyze COD, DO, coliforms, as well as map the depth and chemical composition of the sludge at those points.
Please, we need an exact location to find it on the map, these coordinates 14 ° 29'2'2.3 "90 ° 36'4'0.1" were in the analysis they sent us, but we can't locate them. Also, we need the locations of their analysis from "January to October" if you have.
Thank you for your collaboration and we hope to coordinate as soon as possible. Greetings Doug
Begin forwarded message:

Desde: Grace Corbino <gc@bluefrogsystem.net> Subject: Fw: Inquiries about the bluefrog technologies Date: February 1, 2017 at 4:21:04 PM CST
To: " dougbamboolewis @ gmail. com"< dougbamboolewis@gmail.com>
DC: Brandi Waters <brandi@bluefrogsystem.net>
Desde: Manuel Cano <mcano@amsa.gob.gt> Sent: Wednesday, February 1, 2017 11:36 AM To: Brandi waters
Cc: 'Manuel Cano '
Subject: Inquiries about the bluefrog technologies

 Good day,
I´m in charge of the lake management in lake Amatitlán Guatemala and we are interested to know about the frog system technology
Here, there is a person who sell the equipment (Wastewater Alchemy) and he tell us that the system works with cavitation technologies, but in the specifications of the equipment in your web page is not mentioned.
We want to know if this waste water treatment is an aerator that can be apply in big lakes and if the blue model or any model works with cavitation system Thanks for all and my best regards,
Msc. Manuel Francisco Cano Alfaro
Control, environmental quality and Lake Management
Dear Ing. Juarez and Lic. Cano, cordial greetings.
We have previously sent these documents about our proposal with abundant information and case studies. However, to respond to the request made by Ing. Juárez regarding the explanation of the science that works in our technology, we have dedicated time to prepare this document especially for you. We are at your service for any questions.
We trust that this document will clarify any doubts that Mr. Cano may have regarding how cavitation works in our system and will resolve the concerns that he expressed to our friends at Blue

Frog. We also send you the Operation Manual in Spanish. We can explain in greater detail if you need it at the time you require it.

Sincerely, Douglas Lewis

Dear Amed, we received your request for information and we will be gathering it in a printed version to deliver it to you personally any day of the next week that you indicate to us. However, from your request we conclude that they did not receive the abundant information sent previously (since 2016 and more recently in January 2017), so we will send it to you again in this email. The material clearly explains the function of cavitation within a system that applies various vertically stratified physical and chemical phenomena for the treatment of water, or if it is not clearly explained and you still have doubts about it, please send us the specific questions of the operation and I will answer them with great pleasure.

There are also interesting articles by our manufacturer (Chip Bettle, my uncle, and BlueFrog System) of the equipment we use within our systems that we will gladly translate into Spanish and include in the delivery of documents that we will do next week according to your availability.

Thanks for your interest.

Begin forwarded message:

Desde: Doug Lewis <dougbamboolewis@gmail.com> Subject: Re: Methodology for teams Date:

January 19, 2017 at 10:34:56 AM CST

To: Manuel Cano <manuelfcano@gmail.com>

C c: " oamedjuarez @ hotmail. com" <oamedjuarez@hotmail.com>, ctobar@amsa.gob.gt, Alejandro Arroyave <aarroyave@revistaperrobravo.com>, Daniela Alvarez Schottler <daniela.aldizz@gmail.com>

Good afternoon dear Manuel,

Below I answer some of your questions and attach a document with the scientific explanation of what our technology does. We wait until today Thursday to obtain the laboratory results of the COD analyzes carried out in the area near the installed cavitation machines, we understand that it may take more time so I proceed to comment on the information sent so far, which continues to be scarce.

 - As we can see with the only two measurements sent in relation to the aerators, it is that these do remove but generate more sludge, hence a concentration of 63 mg / L at 1 meter distance and 39 mg / L at 100 meters away. This does not happen with our CAVITATION machines, precisely because they remove sludge. If the sludge were
Moving from one side to the other they would be shown in the concentration of contamination in the water, that is, our COD measurement, in the middle of the machines, between 15 and 10 meters away from the equipment, was much higher than 4.5 mg / L.
- Our technology eliminates sludge transforming that carbon material through the installation of an ecosystem dominated by archaea. As you will understand in the attached document, we want the archaea to dominate the system in such a way that the contamination is translated into pure water, methane and a bottom made up of $CaCO_3$ granules. That is why it is very important not only to measure the depth of the sludge, which will be greatly reduced, but also the mapping of sludge should include analysis of the chemical composition of the bottom, because there we will find that it has changed and, therefore, behaves differently.
- We agree with the methodology that you apply to evaluate the other water treatment projects, but we propose that the reduction of COD and the elimination of sludge be the parameters with which any other proposed treatment is compared. As you can see

in the results they sent us, there is no point that even comes close to the reduction evidenced two weeks after installation.

 CAVITATING machines. We can spend the whole year discussing study methodologies, but we must focus on what is already happening and do everything possible to validate it, for you and so will universities and private laboratories, so that we have all the scientific evidence. available to justify any public investment to clean up the lake.
- You have in your hands, and it is your duty, to collaborate and facilitate the necessary analysis to make transparent what is happening with this pilot, who has shown results that have never been recorded in the history of AMSA. Let's avoid getting complicated and let's be practical in approaching this pilot to be able to objectively evaluate the various
water treatment projects for Lake Amatitlán. We insist: the reduction of COD and the elimination of sludge must be the parameters that determine the quality of the results of this technology, and compared to any other.
We are sure that after reading the attached document, you will be able to understand more easily why the following answers:
- There is no range that "should" exist between sludge and digging equipment. They work whatever that distance.
- The curtains have the purpose of establishing a HRT and maintaining a flow in order to identify the reduction cost per kg of COD. These will be installed from the surface to more than 1 meter deep, joined and without open spaces. No surface or subsurface current will influence that area.

 - We do not think of a minimum HRT, the teams do their work with any HRT, we think rather around obtaining the maximum possible HRT because that implies a lower cost per kg reduced and that is in the interest of taxpayers . Nobody wants to spend

more taxes on more expensive options. We should think around as much HRT as possible to clean more.
- The radius of action of the equipment is very extensive since sine waves are generated that go out in all directions. They must consider that the radius of action where they are installed reaches up to the shores that surround the area.
- We repeat: there is no movement of sludge, there is elimination and transformation.
In conclusion, we agree on the consensus reached with AMSA in our last meeting, for taking samples from 10, 20, 40, 50, 100, 200+ of the machines, towards at least 8 orientations cardinals, to analyze COD, DO, coliforms, as well as mapping the depth and chemical composition of the sludge at these points. Please, we need an exact location to find it on the map, these coordinates 14 ° 29'2'2.3 "90 ° 36'4'0.1" were in the analyzes you sent us, but we cannot locate them. Also, we need the locations of your analyzes from "January to October" if you have.
Thank you for your collaboration and we hope to coordinate as soon as possible.
Regards Doug

 On J an 1 6, 2 0 1 7, at 3: 4 2 PM, Ma nuel Ca no < manuelfcano@gmail.com> wrote:
Good afternoon dear Doug,
By means of this sending information requested from Lake Amatitlán and on Wednesday I hope to transfer the results of the COD and BOD analysis laboratory carried out in an area close to the equipment that you offer.
Regarding the definition of methodologies that may be useful to measure the efficiency of the equipment that Wastewater Alchemy offers, I consider that it is necessary to define it together, through your technical team and technical staff from AMSA and collaborators, for a methodology endorsed by both.

However, analyzing the way of proposing the methodology we
would need complementary information based on:
• Distance range that must exist between the sludge and
digging teams
• Installation way and curtains design to avoid the
subsurface flow of streams
• Minimum residence times that the
water in contact with the equipment
• Radius of action of the equipment for installation •
Bioaugmentation effect that may occur due to
sludge movement
On the other hand, I would appreciate transferring information on
the technical specifications of the
equipment and operating method in open bodies of water, since
the hydrodynamic cavitation processes that I found are

 associated for wastewater. This in order to avoid a bad
experimental design that results in a misinterpretation and
reliability of the information obtained.
Sincerely,
--
Lic. Manuel Francisco Cano
Tel .: 47665365
<Lake January-November.xlsx> <DCA16-032 DougLewis
short.pdf>
Begin forwarded message:
Desde: Doug Lewis <dougbamboolewis@gmail.com>
Subject: most recent analysis (of a pig farm in Mexico)
Date: June 28, 2016 at 10:26:16 AM CST
To: Manuel Cano <manuelfcano@gmail.com>
Hello Manuel,
here is more evidence of the adventures of more residence. This
is from page 10.

don't talk to eric yet. I look forward to your ideas on geomembrane and cleaning the lagoon.
Begin forwarded message:
Desde: Doug Lewis <dougbamboolewis@gmail.com> Subject: amsa presentation

 Date: June 11, 2016 at 7:41:49 PM CST To: oamedjuarez@hotmail.com
. . . . your equipmentONLY airs the water and does NOT do anything else.
Oscar heard them and they state you selected places for the equipment that WERE NOT the HIGHEST
contaminated but the clearest and THEY, HAVE doubts of the efficiency of said equipment.
THEY, say they have given you the agreed on support and the machinery HAS BEEN KEPT active 24 hours a day. NO obstruction to their function.
They also agree to keep sampling the water everyday but manifest their doubts to the authority you say you have, serving those in your Resumé as valid.
SOMETHING VITAL IS for you to prove the sludge IS removed thereof.
I´d advise you get some certificates from all those you´v´e served, as well as their contact info as to expedite these fuckers´´ posture, which is totally against you.
There´s someone else withinthe VP´s circle, that opposes the program saying it may be similiar to the " magic water "
I´m lettting you know about this, because I finally got my meeting with the National Secretary and he´s WORRIED we support your case and get screwed if shit hits the fan and I NEED YOU TO PROVE OTHERWISE PRIOR to the Multicyt petition as to give my friend the Secretary something solid to support your case.
You must understand it is CRUCIAL for all NOT to let those fuckers get away with this criterion against you. Do comment and

provide the valid support that will clarify some of the toxic hints
these petty creatures pose. Regards to Your lady and DO
EVERYTHINGWITH FAITH !!!
Edgar
Edgar herbruger
Inventor Prof. ND
MOBILE :(502) 5799 9759 which I personally answer.
Concyt / Sincyt: 3rd Ave. 13-28 Zone 1 Guatemala City
PBX. 23172600 Ext: Pending NEW number.-
edgarherbruger@gmail.com ** My MAIN Mail
edgarherbruger@yahoo.com
mayanwonderproducts@gmail.com
GUATEMAYAHAS DECIDED NOMORE EXTRACTIVE OPS IN
OUR TERRITORY !!!
Human Rights, Environmental Activist
Member of the Nagoya Protocol Coordination Signatory.Worked
from 2011- 2014 Congress Rati fi ed it Feb.5th 2014 I was
honored, to represent over 500 Guatemalensis Women and Men
that worked alongside for months on the of fi cial document for the
signing of this Protocol
Indigenous Communities Infrastructure Supporter.
Inventor of Phitovitamax and Maya Cuscún and Creator of
the Malnutrition Eradication Integrated Program in 5 Years for
Guatemaya.
Coffee Pulp Biofuels and Org. Fert. Promoter
Active Member of the Association of Inventors è Innovadores de
Guatemala
www.inventoresdeguatemala.com
(Under construction) (UnderConstruction)
http://my.barackobama.com/page/community/post/
edgarherbruger/gGxqV8
Active Member of the Concyt Inventors Commission
Alternate President of the Board of Directors for the period 2013-
March 25th, 2014-16 the Commission of

Inventors of the Sincyt in the Concyt
President of the Sub-Commission for International Scientific
Relations of the Commission of Inventors from April 24, 2014 to
March 2016.
Active Member of the Intersectoral Technical Commission for the
Environment of the Science and Technology System since April
14, 2015. Founding Member of Conama in 1991.-
Invited to Participate in the Sectorial Health Technical
Commission from January 20, 2016.- www.facebook.com/
edgarherbruger tweeter @ edgarherbruger
Wonderful Mayan Products
www.mayanwonderproducts.com (Under Construction)
edgarherbruger@mayanwonderproducts.com
Mayan Wonder Products: This website will be restored and
activated by August 2017. DUE TO FINANCIAL
COMPLICATIONS
CEO - Legal Representative
Condominium Construction Corporation (Under Initial Phase of
Construction and Registration)Projected Phase 1 Projected to be
Concluded By August 2017 DUE TO
FINANCIALCOMPLICATIONS.
June 11, 2017
Oscar Manuel Cobar Pinto, Ph.D.
National Secretary of Science and Technology
CONCYT: 3rd. Ave. 13-28 zone 1
Guatemala City, Guatemala
Dear Secretary,
Thank you very much for your time at last Wednesday's meeting.
It is a pleasure to greet you in this way, I hope everything goes
very well in your activities.
Attached, I send the proposal that we prepared for the pilot in
Lake Amatitlán, a monitoring plan and analysis taking to obtain

the real cost of cleaning the lake. I hope you can read it and comment on your opinion. A cordial greeting.
Doug Lewis.
Relive Amatitlán http://ww.reviveamatitlan.org fb: revive amatitlan
Local phone 45341614
+ 1 415 377 5043 info@reviveamatitlan.org
Received dear Doug, I will read it and react. Greetings. Oscar Cobar